The Silver Arch

# THE STRANGE WORLD OF GURNEY SLADE

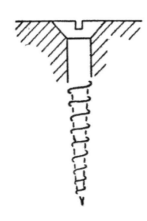

## By Andrew Hickey

THE SILVER ARCHIVE

THE STRANGE WORLD OF GURNEY SLADE

ISBN: 9781913456054


Published by Obverse Books, Edinburgh

Range Editor: Stuart Douglas

Cover Design: Cody Schell

First edition: August 2020

10 9 8 7 6 5 4 3 2 1

Text © 2020 Andrew Hickey

A CIP catalogue record for this title is available from the British Library.

# Contents

Introduction

Chapter 1 - Anthony Newley

Chapter 2 - What is The Strange World of Gurney Slade?

Chapter 3 – Episode One

Chapter 4 - Is Gurney Newley?

Chapter 5 - The Strange World of 1960

Chapter 6- Episode Two

Chapter 7 - On Auteurship

Chapter 8 - On Menippean Satire

Chapter 9 - Episode Three

Chapter 10 - The Running Jumping & Standing Still Film

Chapter 11 - Hancock

Chapter 12 - Episode Four

Chapter 13 - Fairy Tales

Chapter 14 - On the Promos

Chapter 15 - Episode Five

Chapter 16 - The Music of Gurney Slade

Chapter 17 - Episode Six

Chapter 18 - Post-Gurney Works

Bibliography

Biography

# Current Titles

The Silver Archive Special 1: The Christmas Box

- Paul Magrs

The Silver Archive #1: Sapphire & Steel Assignments 1 & 2

- David and Lesley McIntee

The Silver Archive #2: Sapphire & Steel Assignments 3 & 4

- Cody Schell

The Silver Archive #3: Sapphire & Steel Assignments 5 & 6

- James Cooray Smith

The Silver Archive #4: Stranger Things Season 1

- Paul Driscoll

The Silver Archive #5: Dark Skies

- Matthew Kresal

# Overview

Title: The Strange World of Gurney Slade
Writers: Dick Hills, Sid Green, Anthony Newley (uncredited)
Directors: Alan Tarrant, Anthony Newley

Original UK Transmission Dates:    22 October 1960, 8.35pm
                                   29 October 1960, 8.35pm
                                    5 November 1960, 11.10pm
                                   12 November 1960, 11.10pm
                                   19 November 1960, 11.10pm
                                   26 November 1960, 11.10pm

Running Times:                     Six episodes of 30 minutes.

Regular Cast: Anthony Newley (Gurney Slade)

Guest Cast: John Bosh (Frank's Son), Margaret Cox (Frank's Daughter), Ann Lancaster (Dog), Charles Lloyd Pack (Tinker), Edwin Richfield (Husband), Keith Smith (Policeman), Joy Stewart (Wife), Una Stubbs (Girl in Park), Anneke Wills (Girl on Airfield), Douglas Wilmer (Prosecuting Counsel), Bernie Winters (Albert).

Critical Responses:

'One of television's genuine oddities, **The Strange World of Gurney Slade** was a whimsical 'comedy of thought' following one ex- (or so he thinks) actor's meandering journey through a fantasy world.'

[Catriona Wright, 'The Strange World of Gurney Slade', BFI Screenonline]

'While I can admire the gall of it, the pioneering spirit which created it and the bloody-mindedness of both Newley and his writers creating something so wildly off-centre, I'm really not sure whether watching it is an enjoyable experience or an utterly pointless one.'

[Paul Mount, 'DVD Review: The Strange World of Gurney Slade', Starburst Magazine]

# Synopsis

After breaking the fourth wall of a mundane sitcom, **Gurney Slade** walks off stage and out of the television studio, preferring instead to spend six weeks wandering around London and its environs in a series of increasingly surreal adventures, all backgrounded by the sound of his own thoughts.

•

# Introduction

The Silver Archive series exists primarily to discuss science fiction and fantasy series, but those genres can be very broad indeed. In this series we are going to look at obvious candidates like **Buffy the Vampire Slayer**, which are firmly in the centre of the genre as most people understand it, but we'll also be examining work which many might not immediately consider as being part of those genres, but which on closer examination can be seen to fit into them, albeit not always especially comfortably.

**The Strange World of Gurney Slade** is one such. It's a series which few would think of when asked to name fantasy TV, and which has few of the typical markings of genre TV even when judged by the somewhat broader stylistic range that vintage British telefantasy allows, but which is still undoubtedly fantastical and taking place in an unreal world. It might be considered magical realism rather than fantasy per se, but the dividing line between those two genres is more to do with intention of acceptance within the literary canon than with techniques or subject matter. Similarly, one can consider it absurdism, but **The Hitch-Hiker's Guide to the Galaxy** is also absurdist, and there are few who would claim that that series was not science fiction as well[1].

But no matter what genre one chooses to assign it to, **The Strange World of Gurney Slade** is one of the most interesting pieces of television ever created. Appearing right at the start of the postmodern era, before the term had even been applied to anything outside architecture, it subverts the expectations of genre, deconstructs the sitcom, acknowledges the existence of an author separate from the world the characters live in who can manipulate

---

[1] For those who are not familiar with the series, incidentally, perhaps best to turn to the chapter 'What Is The Strange World of Gurney Slade?', which explains in more detail what the series is about, and the basics of what, if any, genre the series belongs to. For the rest of this introduction, we shall be assuming that the reader has at least a passing familiarity with the series.

events within the story, and talks about the commercial realities that limit and shape the form of the story.

Nearly sixty years on from its first broadcast, **The Strange World of Gurney Slade** still looks extraordinarily advanced. At the original time of broadcast – when it was shown on ITV in prime time to a family audience (at least at first, before being unceremoniously moved to a late-night slot once the programme controllers realised what it actually was) – it must have seemed like something from another planet.

Because **The Strange World of Gurney Slade** is a series which has its roots in 1950s popular culture, but which preempts much of what was considered innovative in the later 1960s. Watching it now, it is easy to see elements of *A Hard Day's Night*, of **The Prisoner**, of **Q5** and **Monty Python's Flying Circus**, of **Doctor Who** stories like *The Mind Robber*... in short, it's easy to see much of what is distinctive about the TV and cinema of the 1960s making its first appearance here.

And that's not what you'd expect from a series that was meant to be a family sitcom, starring a pop star, and written by the people who are now best known for writing for Morecambe and Wise before Eddie Braben replaced them. It certainly wasn't what the people in charge expected when it was commissioned.

So, in this book we will look at how the most forward-looking piece of TV from a forward-looking age was created by people who one would normally be expecting to be making something far more forgettable, and how that ultimately stems from the unique nature of Anthony Newley as an artist – as well as what the likely contributions of the show's actual writers were.

Normally in sitcom (and **The Strange World of Gurney Slade** is, at least nominally, a sitcom) the auteur, to the extent that there is one, is the writer – sitcom is a writer's medium, and even in the case of shows based around a non-writing lead actor (such as **Hancock**, of which much more later), the tone of the show is set by the writers – **Hancock** was far more about the vaguely melancholic tone that Galton and Simpson brought to the scripts than it was about anything that Tony Hancock himself did, wonderful as Hancock's performance undoubtedly was (as can be seen by comparing the later work for both writers and actor). Yet in the case of **The Strange World of Gurney Slade**, everything about the series centres on Anthony Newley, and it's to his work that one needs to look to find a context for the series.

Newley is, as we shall see, a strange figure – one who managed to be a massive influence on the culture as a whole while, for the most part, staying on the fringes. He's someone whose songs are known by almost everyone, yet who is rarely thought of as a songwriter. He was a filmmaker who Roger Ebert compared to Fellini and Godard, but that comparison was made about a sex comedy with characters called Polyester Poontang and Filigree Fondle. He was best known for his appearances on game shows and spent his last years working on soap operas, yet he was someone with a serious artistic intent. It's very hard to think of a figure in British popular culture who exemplified and embraced more different and contradictory personae, while integrating them successfully.

And **The Strange World of Gurney Slade** absolutely fits into his work – it's recognisably a creation of the same mind as *Stop The World I Want To Get Off* and *Can Hieronymus Merkin Ever Forget Mercy Humppe And Find True Happiness?* – but it's also very much a product of its time. It has its roots in the pop-existentialism of the late fifties, in the work of people like Colin Wilson, but also in the way that work leached into the broader popular culture. We've already mentioned Tony Hancock (and he will be coming up many more times in this book), but the attitudes shown in Hancock's film *The Rebel* exemplify the way this sense of alienation, combined with a belief in an ill-defined specialness on the part of young and middle-aged British men of the time, had become deeply rooted in the popular culture.

Not everyone was reading Wilson, but everyone was watching Hancock, and the two weren't so far apart.

So, this book will take **The Strange World of Gurney Slade** in its cultural context. We'll look at it as a forerunner of the films of Richard Lester and the comedy of Monty Python, but also as something inspired by the Angry Young Men and Galton and Simpson. But within that, we'll also look at what it is that makes this still a valuable piece of TV today – at what it does with narrative structure and self-referentiality, at the ideas it uses and the techniques it pioneered. And we'll look in detail at the ways in which it points to a more expansive definition of televised fantasy and science fiction than the one that many people think of – because just as this series is indeed a part of a particular existentialist tradition, and just as it's part of a particular sitcom tradition, it's also part of a tradition that includes **Doctor Who**, **The Box of Delights**, **The Prisoner**, and many more of the greats of British telefantasy over the years.

This is a tradition of metafictional narrative, of the fantastic used to satirise contemporary society. It's a tradition in which the boundaries between the fantastic and the real are blurred, and metaphor abuts mimetic realism often in the same shot. In these stories, which draw as much from Menippean satire as they do from the works that are more normally considered to be science fiction or fantasy, the world is a strange place into which characters and situations from other narratives can intrude, and in which the imagination is reified.

The roots of **Gurney Slade** can be found as much in *Gulliver's Travels* as in any more obvious antecedents – the series is part of a long tradition – but at the same time it's a series that could only have been made in 1960.

**Gurney Slade** is an individualistic work by a particular individual, and also a work that required many people's input and could only have been made in a particular culture. It's a work that is *sui generis* but which is also part of multiple genres. And over the course of this book we will look at those contradictions and see how – and if – we can resolve them. To start with, let's take a closer look at the man behind Gurney...

# Chapter 1 - Anthony Newley

Anthony Newley is one of the strangest figures in British popular culture – someone who seemed determined to make personal, important art, while working in the most frivolous and ephemeral of media, and for a giant popular audience. Given those constraints, his career is a remarkable one, and taking a broad look at his body of work, Newley was something of a renaissance man.

He had started as an actor, appearing as a child star in David Lean's 1948 version of *Oliver Twist* as the Artful Dodger, before becoming one of Britain's most popular leading men in his early adulthood. He'd then made a sudden side-swerve into pop stardom, more or less by chance, after being cast in the 1959 film *Idol on Parade* as an Elvis-like pop star who had been drafted into the army (as the real Elvis had at the time).

Newley had sung the songs for the film, and had unexpected chart success – suddenly, he was something of a teen idol, competing with the likes of Tommy Steele and Marty Wilde for the affections of teenage girls across the UK. He became a pop star, and one of the first pop stars to sing with a British accent rather than affecting a pseudo-American one. On hearing Newley's early pop singles now, one is immediately struck by how much of an influence he was on David Bowie, whose early work amounted to vocal clones of Newley's style[2]. But Bowie isn't the only musician to be influenced by Newley – Bowie's namesake Davy Jones (of the Monkees), the Kinks, Madness, Blur, all owed a great deal to Newley's particular Cockney theatricalism.

But Newley, unlike most of the pop stars of the day, wasn't content merely to be a singer. He became one of Britain's great singer-songwriters, collaborating with Leslie Bricusse on a variety of

---

[2] "I was the world's worst mimic...I was Anthony Newley for a year." (Bowie, NME, 1973)

songs that became standards and are known by everyone, usually without them even realising that they were written by Newley.

And when I say known by everyone, I mean known by everyone. There's 'Feeling Good', the song that was a hit for Nina Simone and later for Muse. There's 'Gonna Build a Mountain', which became a success for Sammy Davis Jr. And then there's his songs for films, like all the songs for *Willy Wonka and the Chocolate Factory*, or the theme from *Goldfinger*.

Newley was more successful in his *third* most successful career than almost anyone is even in a career they put their life into.

During his time, Newley was a maker of experimental music ('Moogies Bloogies', with Delia Derbyshire of the BBC Radiophonic Workshop, is a particularly interesting example of early-60s electronica), a star of stage and screen, an award-winning screenwriter, a director, and a songwriter. Yet he's probably best known now for having been a regular on **Hollywood Squares** in the US for much of the 70s, and for his performance in **EastEnders** during the last years of his life.

But we're not looking at those last years right now. We're looking at 1960, when Newley was a film star who had also become a pop star and a successful TV variety performer. At this point in his career, he had given no indication of being any more interesting a figure than, say, Jim Dale or Tommy Steele, other light-entertainment figures who worked in multiple media.

And one of the media Newley worked in was, of course, TV. In particular, in early 1960 he worked on a TV show called **Saturday Spectacular**. That show, which ran from 1956 to 1961, was one of ATV's most popular shows. This series gave popular entertainers their own episodes (and so Newley's episodes were titled *Saturday Spectacular Presents The Anthony Newley Show*, for example) but working with a regular production team. These were variety shows involving songs, sketches, and general all-round entertainment.

Among the people who regularly worked on **Saturday Spectacular** were scriptwriters Dick Hills and Sid Green, who were until 1959 the writers for comedian Dave King, but who were also jobbing comedy writers. Their work on **Saturday Spectacular** was later to lead them to their greatest fame, as writers (and occasional on-screen stooges) on Morecambe and Wise's first hit TV series, **Two of a Kind**, which was to debut the next year, also on ATV, after the double-act also appeared on **Saturday Spectacular**.

But at this point in their career, Hills and Green were no better known than any other writers. Their main strength was an ability to write material in a comedian's established voice – a useful talent when coming up with sketches and routines at short notice for many different acts.

Newley, however, was not content with them merely providing him material to perform – he wanted to collaborate with them, at least on the ideas if not on the complete scripts, and so the three worked together on the material that became Newley's TV show. And one of the ideas that the three came up with went down surprisingly well – they wrote a simple sketch, in which Newley and other performers would talk together, but at the same time, the audience would hear a pre-recorded tape of the characters' thoughts, which would provide an amusing juxtaposition with the words they actually said.

The audience loved it, and the popularity of the idea inspired Hills, Green, and Newley to come up with a new series, in which you would be able to hear the main character's thoughts all the time.

And that's where we come in.

# Chapter 2 - What is The Strange World of Gurney Slade?

It might seem unusual for a book about a specific TV series to contain an explanation as to what that TV series actually is, but **The Strange World of Gurney Slade** is an unusual TV series. If nothing else, very few people under the age of sixty can have any memory at all of seeing it on TV. It was broadcast in 1960, repeated in 1963, and then (other than one 1992 repeat of a single episode) never shown again, so only those who have bought the 2011 Network DVD of the series on the basis of its cult reputation will have any idea what the series actually involves. Given that this book is part of a series on different TV shows, it must be presumed that at least some of this book's readers are people who are buying the whole **Silver Archive** series and don't necessarily have any awareness of the programme. This chapter is aimed, mostly, at those readers.

So, to sum up, **The Strange World of Gurney Slade** was a six-episode series, a star vehicle for Anthony Newley. It was broadcast in late 1960, starting off in a prime-time slot but quickly moving to a late-night one as the ratings fell off a cliff-edge and the complaints started to come in. It details the thoughts of a character, the eponymous Gurney Slade, as he wanders around and encounters an increasingly fantastical set of situations and environments.

**The Strange World of Gurney Slade** is a sitcom. Or at least, it was billed as a sitcom, and in its first few minutes it even looked like being one, but it's not a series that goes for jokes first and foremost, as opposed to being a witty exploration of ideas, and it has far more in common with *Alice in Wonderland* (especially Jonathan Miller's 1966 adaptation) than anything normally termed a sitcom.

Earlier in 1960, in a variety TV special, Anthony Newley had performed in sketches in which people would have conversations while their inner monologues would be heard by the audience as voiceover, contradicting or putting a different spin on the things they were saying.

This was an unusual level of trickery for the time period (a period, remember, in which very few TV shows were made anything other than as live, and in which many were indeed broadcast live rather than pre-recorded), and the sketches proved immensely popular – so popular that it was thought it would be worth putting together a TV series based around the concept.

And, indeed, the first three episodes of **The Strange World of Gurney Slade** are dominated by Newley's voiceover as Gurney Slade's inner monologue – and episode one even has a scene which comes directly from those sketches, in which Gurney and a businessman share a car, with Gurney wondering what impressive thoughts must be going through the other man's head as he makes momentous decisions, while the businessman is merely having sexual fantasies about his mistress. (There is also a smaller echo of this in the second episode's courtship-ritual scenes).

But the series quickly evolved into something very different, and very much more interesting. This became apparent from the very first scene in episode one, where what looks like a typical family sitcom starts to unravel as Newley first doesn't say his lines, prompting confusion from the cast (again, a kind of confusion that would happen on occasion in this time period, and would usually be handled in much the same way that it's handled in the show) before just walking off the sets and into the street.

From this point on, the series gets further and further away from sitcom, and indeed from any recognisable genre at all. The first three episodes are spent watching the character Gurney Slade explore three different environments (the streets of London, an airfield and some areas of suburbia, and a farm in the countryside) and interacting with people, many of whom appear to exist only in his imagination, as we hear his thoughts about society in voiceover.

Then, just as the series seems to have established this as a style, everything changes again. The last three episodes of the series are all studio-bound, and in some ways seem closer to conventional sitcom – they're all based on dialogue, and many of the characters are recognisable types who would have been familiar from other sitcoms (and indeed Gurney himself seems to be based on one of those types, as we discuss later). But while those episodes are based on character interaction, they're also about the exploration of fantastical spaces and ideas, whether that be the Gurneyland inside Gurney's own mind or the grotesque, Kafkaesque, courtroom in which all of episode four takes place.

All of this is shot in ways that go against sitcom convention – there's no studio audience, it's shot on film rather than on videotape, and while there are definitely laugh-out-loud funny moments, there's rather more which is just about exploration of ideas and riffing, in ways which may seem surprisingly modern to those who don't have a firm grasp on the history of comedy. The discussion of ants carrying grand pianos in their mandibles in episode three, for example, is pure Eddie Izzard, in content if not in delivery, although it owes a great deal to the house style of Associated London Scripts[3].

The series was massively influential – David Bowie cited it in interviews as an influence on him (as Newley more generally influenced him, of course), and one can see its fingerprints all over shows as diverse as **The Prisoner** (especially the famous final episode, which is spookily similar to the final episode of *Gurney*), **Monty Python's Flying Circus** (Eric Idle has listed 'Anthony Newley in The Small [sic]World of Gurney Slade' in a list of his influences[4]), and even arguably **Hancock** – but it remained almost entirely unknown, because the public reception of the series was so bad.

Looking at it now, it's clear just how much of the innovative TV and film of the late 1960s was presaged here. Episode one of Gurney Slade contains some shots which are almost identical to sequences in *A Hard Day's Night*, whose director wasn't even to make his first feature film (the less-celebrated *It's Trad, Dad!*) for another two years (although it's fair to point out that that director, Richard Lester,

---

[3] A writers' cooperative that produced much of the most influential comedy of the late 50s and early sixties. As far as I know no-one involved in *Gurney Slade* worked with ALS, but ALS' writers were responsible for so much comedy at that time, and in particular so much of the comedy that other writers admired, that it's possible to see the ALS style even in works like *Gurney Slade* which had no formal connection to them.

[4] Idle, Eric, 'Influences', http://www.ericidle.com/blog/2016/04

had worked with Spike Milligan and Peter Sellers on projects such as *The Running, Jumping, and Standing Still Film*, which may well itself have exerted more than a little influence on **Gurney Slade**, especially on episode two).

What we have in **The Strange World of Gurney Slade** is, essentially, the moment when many strands that had been present in 1950s British culture – in **Hancock's Half Hour** and the *Molesworth* books, **The Goon Show** and *Absolute Beginners*, John Osborne plays and Colin Wilson books – all started to come together and flower into the 1960s of **Python**, the Beatles, **Doctor Who** and **The Prisoner**. But it's not just a series that's interesting as a missing link in cultural evolution. This is still a series with a lot to say, and whose last episode, in particular, is an example of conceptual horror that has rarely, if ever, been bettered on British TV.

But this is a sitcom with no fixed situation and with little emphasis on comedy. Over the course of this book we will look at what the series is actually doing, and why sitcom is not perhaps the best label for it, but that was how it was initially promoted, and when people sat down to watch the first episode that's what they were expecting.

# Chapter 3 – Episode One

Episode one is in some ways the odd episode out for **Gurney Slade** – because it was broadcast as part of *TV Heaven* in 1992, for nearly twenty years it was the only episode of the series to which most people had any access, thanks to off-air tapes of that broadcast. As a result, it was the episode which, up until the Network DVD release of the series in 2011, shaped the perception of the series, at least among that small number of people who thought about it at all.

Luckily, it doesn't give as much of an incorrect impression as most first episodes of series – it clearly sets out most of the themes and preoccupations which will dominate the other five episodes of the series. Indeed, had episode two or three been the episodes broadcast in the 90s, the series would likely have had a much less accurate public memory, as they have far fewer of the series' characteristic attributes.

We start with what seems to be a fairly standard sitcom of the time. Mrs Padgett is doing the ironing and complaining to her husband Albert about his laziness. Little Alfie is trying to study for his eleven-plus, Albert's mother lives with them, and there's a pedantic lodger (coded as someone who's possibly autistic[5], and who is certainly prim and proper) and a comedy fat Northern neighbour, Mr Ramsbotham. The jokes are the usual predictable sort of thing for the kind of series this appears to be:

MRS PADGETT

He's training to be an insanitary spectre.

---

[5] At the time this would not have been how this coding was thought of; but there are recognisable types in fiction with attributes that correspond to ones often seen in autistic people – who have, of course, existed since long before an official diagnosis was possible.

MR HOPKINS

No, Mrs P, sanitary inspector!

MRS PADGETT

Oh, have you changed your job then?

The social place of each of these characters is set up immediately by their dress, manner of speech, and attitudes. Mr Hopkins the lodger is wearing a turtleneck jumper, while Mr Ramsbotham has trousers pulled up over his large waist and braces. Albert, on the other hand, wears a suit and tie, of a cut that was ultra-fashionable at the time (it looks very similar to the suits the Beatles would wear in their earliest TV appearances, though it has a more obvious collar). Meanwhile, Albert's mother is such a recognisable type that the only surprising thing about her is that they didn't get Irene Handl to play her, as it felt that Handl played essentially the same character, or a similar one, in almost every British film or TV series from 1954 to 1970 inclusive.

It becomes apparent relatively quickly that this is deliberate – that these characters are so broadly drawn, and such obvious types, in order to parody the standard tropes of late-50s and early-60s sitcom. But at first, it seems that this is just an example of such a sitcom, and not a particularly interesting example. A modern viewer unaware of what's coming might be tempted to turn off, singularly unimpressed with this weak material, were it not for a couple of odd points.

One is that there's no laugh track, unlike virtually every sitcom of its type. The other is that Albert, Anthony Newley's character, seems as unimpressed with the show he's in as the viewer.

And Albert starts to get more and more annoyed. Were it not for the fact that Albert is played by star of stage, screen, and disc Anthony Newley, we probably wouldn't notice that he doesn't seem to be acting as broadly as everyone else, and that he hasn't yet had any lines.

But we do notice that, and we notice more that when Albert does get a line, he doesn't say it.

This wasn't completely unusual in late fifties and early 1960's television. Actors would occasionally miss a cue and have to be prompted, as most TV series were made as live, even when they were pre-recorded – videotape editing posed massive technical challenges, as well as rendering the tape unusable for future programmes, and so the practice at the time was just to keep going if an actor messed up.

But Newley is prompted, over and over again, with his line 'a boiled egg for me, my love', and says nothing. As the prompter keeps whispering the line, Newley pulls on a coat. The rest of the characters vamp, increasingly desperately, as he gives no sign of wanting to say his line. We start to see boom mics, and then Newley/Albert walks off the set. We pull back, seeing the cameras and studio, and the people trying to get him to stay (including a floor manager played by a very young Geoffrey Palmer)

We've also, though, pulled away from the viewpoint we had originally. Everything we've seen so far has been shot multi-camera[6], but now we're cutting to single-camera film.

"Albert" walks out on to the street, pursued by Palmer, still trying to persuade him to turn back. 'You must be mad! We're on the air!'

"Albert" walks on, unspeaking, though dancing a little jig. The only sound is the theme music for the series, which starts up – and Newley plays air piano to it, as if he knows that even though he's walked off the set he's still on TV. The titles come up – at one point saying "THE WORLD OF STRANGE" before settling into the correct title, and Newley walks on. What he doesn't do is offer any explanation for his decision to walk off the set.

---

[6] Or at least it is shot *as if* on multi-camera videotape. The picture looks, throughout, as if it were shot on film, but the camera techniques used in these early shots are ones that would usually be used in videotaped studio work. Resolution of TV sets in this period was not high enough that audiences would have noticed the difference in stock.

Indeed, it's not until more than five minutes into the episode that we hear Anthony Newley's voice at all. Before we do, we get a scene eerily premonitory of *A Hard Day's Night*, with Newley playing football with a stone he finds on the floor, shot almost identically to the famous scenes of Ringo Starr walking by the canal in the later film. And the stone is the next 'character' to speak, and the first sign that we're into a world that doesn't obey the normal laws of nature, when Newley tries to cast the stone into the river, and the stone shouts 'Oy, you know I can't swim, I'd sink like a stone!'

And only then, after Newley sits down, five minutes and fourteen seconds into the episode, do we hear him speak – or at least, we hear his interior monologue, as he thinks to himself 'A half-hour television show. Half an hour to put the world right. What can you do in half an hour? I need at least forty minutes.'

I won't continue to describe every detail of the first episode (and will describe the later episodes in less detail as well) – much of the rest of it doesn't need a great deal in the way of description, being a mixture of comedy involving the dissonance between what Gurney is thinking and what other people are thinking, and ruminations on thumbing lifts in long-distance lorries and how he should just make up a new language with words like 'Formansville', 'klapotchk', 'spingleholt' and 'flangewick'.

But the monologue at the end of the episode is worth repeating here – Gurney's thoughts as he walks off into the distance after having seen the rest of the cast from the beginning of the episode all watching his current behaviour on the TV.

'I am a walking television show. I can't get away from them. Big Brother's watching me. And Big Dad and Big Mum. The whole family's watching me, I'm like a goldfish in a bowl. I'm a poor squirming squingle under a microscope. Leave me alone will you? I've got a right to me privacy. I just walked out of all this. I don't want to know. Now leave me alone! Switch me off! I've got a right to me own privacy! I'm gonna live me own life! Switch orf! Will you stop it and leave me alone? Go back! Don't follow me will you? There ought to be a law! This is a free country and I shouldn't have to have this problem! Now leave me alone! I warned you, I'll get the law on you!'

All of this (and other events such as his brief romance with Una Stubbs' character from an advertising poster, and his attempts to get rid of the resulting vacuum cleaner) makes this episode almost a microcosm of the whole series – all the major themes of the series appear here.

So, while the series does go to many more interesting places after this, anyone for whom this was the first exposure to the series, whether in 1960, 1963, 1992, or 2011, will have been able to get a very good idea of what they were in for from this.

But in other ways the episode is slightly out of the ordinary for the series, at least in so far as a series like this can have an 'ordinary'. For a start, there's little of the sense of pushing against sexual convention there that we see in the next few episodes, and indeed in Newley's other works along these lines. Some of the thoughts he overhears hint at this slightly – "If only I'd had my teeth in at the time," and "If I showed her those photographs I've got, perhaps she'd be a little more inclined to..." – but it's not a major theme of the episode in the way it is later. There's more of a boundary between fantasy and reality, as we see that no-one other than Gurney can see Una Stubbs' dancing girl, where in later episodes that boundary is more permeable (for example the children in episode two can see the fairy), and there's a persistent sense that what we're watching here is not the adventures of a character called Gurney Slade, but of an actor called Anthony Newley.

The opening few minutes are what's crucial here – Gurney/Newley breaking the fourth wall, but not completely breaking down the barriers between the audience and the show. Gurney walks off from the TV show he's meant to be doing, but as he walks off he plays air piano which provides the soundtrack for the titles, and at the end of the episode he addresses the audience and acknowledges that he's still part of a TV series. When Gurney walks off the set, he's not walking out of his TV series, but walking *into* it – and indeed, we later see the characters who were part of Gurney's sitcom watching the show on TV. Watching, that is, the show we're watching.

The conventional way of interpreting the opening scene, in other words, is only one of two ways of interpreting it. One is that what we're seeing at the start is a rather bland TV show and the actor playing one of the roles walks off the set and into real life. Another is that we're watching bland *real people*, and that one of them walks off *into a TV show*, which the others later watch.

Of course, in the world of the series, both of these interpretations are absolutely true. The narrative levels in the first episode act as a figure/ground illusion, where neither way of watching the episode is more valid than another. But the latter – that Gurney is entering, not exiting, a TV series – is a far more productive way of watching the episode, as it provides a context in which the rest of the series can be viewed, even if it's not the reading that most people jump to immediately.

Indeed, the world through which Gurney wanders is a televisual one – one where people's thoughts can be heard as voiceover, and even one where, in the middle of the story, an advertisement intrudes on the reality of the story. The most important thing to note about **The Strange World of Gurney Slade** might also be the most obvious – that it is a television show.

But we also have, in microcosm, the whole *thematic* story of the series. The series as a whole is about encouraging people to break out of their social scripts, as Gurney does at the beginning, but those people over and over again find that they're still trapped by a greater script, as Gurney does at the end of the episode, as he walks off ranting and asking for his privacy and for the audience to leave him alone – even though he may have left his TV show, he's still in a TV show. Society is something you can't escape, and even nonconformity is just another way of conforming, just to a different set of expectations.

It's also, very clearly, centred around Gurney/Newley. Some later episodes have Gurney interacting with other characters who drive the plot (such as it is), but here he's basically only interacting with himself and with characters in his imagination who appear and disappear more or less at random. The only character who both affects Gurney's actions and seems to exist in the real world (or at least in the level of reality in which the viewer is meant to be understanding the programme) is the policeman – he makes Gurney pick up the newspaper and carry it, rather than drop it on the floor, and this is literally the closest anyone in Gurney's own level of reality comes to affecting his behaviour.

One might say that this episode of **Gurney Slade** is the ultimate in solipsism, with other people either existing only in his imagination (the girl from the advert, the people in the dustbins, the talking dog) or existing in reality and being irritants (the audience, the other characters in the sitcom at the beginning, the policeman). The one exception is Sir Geoffrey Jerome, who is presented as a real-world figure who Gurney admires. Even he, though, turns out to be a totally different person in his own mind from the one that Gurney perceives him as – thinking only about sex (in much the same terms that Gurney himself would use later in the series) rather than thinking about saving the national economy as Gurney imagines him to be.

So when reality impinges on Gurney's life, it's only as an annoyance – yet at the same time the interpretation one might put on the opening sequence is that Gurney *wants* more reality – and certainly while the actions he takes and the characters he interacts with are surreal (in the literal sense of the term rather than the vernacular one), from the moment he steps foot off the TV studio set every location he enters is a real place – the entire episode is shot on film, on location, rather than being shot in the studio on video.

So Gurney has journeyed into reality, taken a look at it, and essentially said, 'I don't like it, I want something better'. This is where the rest of the series goes, of course, as it picks at assumptions both societal and ontological and tries to look at what that something better might be, yet in the end Gurney always remains confined, and both he and everyone else he tries to help escape from the scripts of society ends up reduced to following them anyway, and if anything even worse off. Gurney at the end of episode one (if, indeed, it is "Gurney") is someone who has escaped from a fiction but knows he's still in a fiction – he's a character who is hemmed in by the format but *knows* he's hemmed in by the format. He's gained gnosis, but that gnosis just means that he's aware of the limits that people who don't have his enlightened state don't see.

We only see much later on just what that means for Gurney in terms of being able, or otherwise, to move between levels of reality more freely, and exactly how aware he is of his own fictional nature (when watching the first episode it's perfectly reasonable to assume that he knows he's on TV but doesn't know he's fictional – he might imagine that he's part of some sort of documentary, for example). But even here, in the first episode, the axioms from which everything in the rest of the series follows are laid down.

The series is, as I mentioned earlier, a series of two parts, but episode one manages to bridge the two parts rather more effectively than one might imagine. Structurally and visually, it's definitely part of the first half – episodes two and three follow the same formula of 'Gurney wanders around on location, impinges slightly if at all on the experiences of real people, and interacts a little with people who exist only in his imagination' – but thematically its concerns are not picked up again until episodes four, five, and six, the studio-bound episodes which are structurally and visually utterly different to the first half of the series.

The first episode was both a ratings and a critical success. It got an audience of approximately 12.5 million viewers and received rave reviews from the critics. Unfortunately, it did not receive rave reviews from the lay audience. The episode generated a huge number of complaints from viewers who were not comfortable with it.

The writers had clearly anticipated this – we will see, in episodes four and six especially, what they thought the reaction to the series would be (the entire series was filmed before the first episode was broadcast), but they probably hadn't anticipated the extent of the drop in the ratings – it went from around 12.5 million viewers for episode one to only 8.5 million for episode two. After this ratings drop, further episodes were consigned to a late-night slot.

# Chapter 4 - Is Gurney Newley?

One question that needs to be asked in the context of **The Strange World of Gurney Slade** is 'to what extent is Gurney Slade meant to be Anthony Newley himself?'

This is a more important question than it might at first appear. After all, Gurney is obviously a character that Newley is playing, isn't he?

Well, isn't he?

It's actually a question to which it's basically impossible to give a straightforward answer. We will look here at the evidence, but that evidence is much less conclusive than it appears.

To start with, there's a question of who the actor is in the first scene of episode one. The character being played is not Gurney Slade there – he's even referred to by name as Albert Padgett within the brief sitcom within a sitcom. So the character who leaves the studio and goes walking through London – the character we know as Gurney Slade – is an actor who has a starring role in a TV show (and he is clearly set up as the central figure in that brief scene), just like Anthony Newley is.

And then, when Gurney steals the newspaper in the first episode, the newspaper refers to him as 'Anthony Newley', by name. The article, under the headline 'Can't You Afford Twopence Halfpenny', has a subheading which reads (apart from the words covered up by Newley's thumb in the shot) 'Mr Anthony Newley the well-known man about 27 was seen [thumb]ng a newspaper [thumb] a stand as he was [thumb] away, trying to [thumb] his mind off [thumb]oaeds...'

So there is, at least at the beginning of the series, a deliberate elision between the character 'Gurney Slade' and the actor 'Anthony Newley'. Gurney is not referred to by his own name in the first episode, *is* referred to by Newley's name (but in print, and in a shot that's so brief that viewers would not be expected to read it, especially on the lower-definition TVs of the early sixties), and has the same job as Newley.

These things, however, all change over the course of the series, until we get to the last episode where Newley and Slade are clearly very distinct characters within the fictional world of the TV series – though we should again make the distinction between Anthony Newley the actor and Anthony Newley the character played by Anthony Newley the actor.

So by the end of the series we've had multiple different iterations of Gurnewley, and multiple layers on which he exists. We've had Albert Padgett in the show within a show, played by Gurney-who-is-called-Newley, who is the same character as Gurney Slade, who is not the same character as Anthony Newley, who is a character in the series. And we have Anthony Newley the actor, who plays all of them, and who shares a job with Gurney.

Of course, this elision of multiple levels of narrative is part of the point, but it's interesting to wonder exactly how intentional it was that there would be, for example, multiple Anthony Newleys within the story – did Hills, Green, and Newley have the idea for the last episode in mind when writing the first, or was the original intention for Gurney himself to be Newley in a more direct sense – was this intended to show 'the real Anthony Newley, with only the names changed', or was Gurney intended as a separate character who just had some similarities with Newley's public persona?

Of course, the answer is probably 'all of the above'. While **The Strange World of Gurney Slade** does have a fair amount of narrative coherence – characters and situations from early episodes reappear and are referenced in later ones – it's clearly not engaged in the kind of internally consistent worldbuilding that one generally expects from other telefantasy series. There is no reason at all to think that the character of Gurney can't be at one moment a mouthpiece for the actor playing him, at another a totally separate character, and at a third some halfway point between the two. One of the great strengths of non-realist fiction, after all, is that it allows for this kind of ambiguity, and for questions that are neither resolved nor resolvable (and, in general, speculative fiction is at its weakest when it insists on a kind of encyclopaedic completeness, removing all gaps and ambiguities within the narrative in favour of a series of fictional facts).

While it's unlikely that anyone watching the opening episode of **Gurney Slade** on first broadcast will have noticed the text in the newspaper – and if they did, since he is not referred to by that name in the first episode it would be reasonable to think that the character Newley was playing was called 'Anthony Newley', in the same way that Tony Hancock played a character called 'Tony Hancock' – it is interesting that even that early on the production team were planting the question in the episodes. This ambiguity is aided by the fact that there are no character names in the credits of any episode – the actors are credited, but there is no way to tell from the broadcast credits alone who played what, or what the names of the characters were.

The character does refer to himself as 'Mr. Slade', in passing, in his own interior monologue in episode two (and later in episode three) but in that episode he is also able to create another copy of himself, who looks identical, but who is happy to go off with a coded-as-unattractive woman who has fallen in love at first sight with the real Gurney – 'lucky I carry a spare'. This does not, perhaps, suggest a conception of identity which matches with the normal one. And so at this point we have had two Slades, a Newley, and a character-played-by-Slade-or-Newley. And we're only half way through episode two.

As with many of the questions surrounding the narrative, it's one that then takes a back seat for episodes two and three, as we move into the slower-paced, less interesting parts of the narrative (and I suspect that one reason for the lack of success of the series is that these two episodes were seen before the much more fascinating back half of the series). In episode three Gurney refers to himself as Slade in an interior monologue, but also points out that Gurney Slade (the name of a real place, shown on a signpost in that episode) is an odd name – without saying that it's his own name. As of the end of episode three we have no mentions of Slade's name by anyone else, and only two mentions of it in his interior monologue. Given the lack of character credits in any of the episodes, it would be entirely reasonable for someone watching who hadn't caught those two brief references to think that this was not a character called Gurney Slade at all.

It's not until episode four that we have another character actually refer to Gurney Slade by name – and it's interesting that this starts to happen only as the series descends into its metafiction, and characters start to take on a more obviously prismatic aspect, being separated and recombined into multiple versions of themselves. Slade has always had that aspect – see again the spare Slade in episode two – but now it becomes massively more obvious.

In episode four, after all, we have the TV show on trial, but Gurney *also* being one of the jurors, as well as the defendant and a character in the TV show (and the TV show we see is not an excerpt from an episode that was ever made or broadcast – it's in the style of the series we see, but it's not from it). In episode five, for the first time, we explicitly have Newley playing multiple characters – there's a devil-horned version of Gurney representing his evil side, Gurney's depression, and an unnamed Newley-played character who performs Newley's contemporaneous hit 'Strawberry Fair', which Gurney then comments on disparagingly, but in a way that suggests that he and the performer are the same person even though Gurney is in the audience while the performer sings on stage.

But most interestingly, in the early part of episode five, our principal character tries to tell kids about 'Gurneyland', and the power of the imagination, but he gets annoyed when the children think 'Gurneyland' is in *his* specific, mind, and decamp there. There's a clear implication here that perhaps 'Gurneyland' (and thus 'Gurney') shouldn't be identified with an individual, but is a mode of thinking.

And in this world, after all, it is possible for a single character to be embodied by multiple people – the fairy played by Hugh Paddick in episode two is clearly the same character as the fairy played by Graham Stark in episode six. Nothing is stated in the episodes themselves, but it's certainly possible to interpret identity in this series as almost a process of metempsychosis, that different people can take on different identities at different times, and different identities can be embodied by different people.

Most interesting, perhaps, is the split between creator and creation in episode six, and this is something we're going to look at a lot during the course of this book. Gurney, not Newley, is here treated as the 'author' of the TV series, and is also pointed to as a 'performer' (note, not a character) at the opening. Newley is presented as Gurney's creator, but Gurney himself is the creator of all the other characters in the series – and both Newley and Gurney are ultimately under the control of a mysterious director, but in reality the uncredited director of the series was Newley himself.

It's important to note, as well, that Gurney Slade is, all the way through, a consistent performance, and one made up of deliberate decisions on Newley's part. When we see 'Anthony Newley' appear, at the end of episode six (and also in episode five as the singer), his body language, tone of voice, and hair style are different enough that we can instantly tell the difference between him and Gurney. The devilish version of Gurney who appears in episode five is different again – while Gurney's body language and facial expressions are very reserved, the devil's are animated (and more than a little camp). It's a far more physical performance – or at least it appears to be, because of course it shows that the apparent restraint in Gurney's physical characterisation is *also* a physical performance choice. Newley is clearly, at different points, blurring and sharpening the lines between these different characterisations, but they are different ones.

Now, none of this is conclusive of course, and in many ways that's the point. **The Strange World of Gurney Slade** absolutely resists anything which might seem conclusive. One thing we'll see over and again in this book is that there is no key to unlock what this series is about or what is real in it, and if you were hoping for one, you'll probably be disappointed and should probably stop reading now. But we *can* ask the question 'what is happening at this particular point?

And if we do that, we see something almost like a birth of a separate character here – over the six episodes, Gurney starts as being identical to Newley, even sometimes sharing his name, and then slowly becomes a distinct character, with his own name, desires, drives, and motivations, only to be packed up and carried away at the very end, deprived once again of all his individuality, with his characteristics, such as they are, reabsorbed into his creator.

One of the many things the series is doing is pointing out the difference between fictional personas and real people, and in the end, it's possibly best to take Gurney as being Anthony Newley – but not Anthony Newley the real person; rather Anthony Newley the public persona. Newley would make many attempts to leave that persona behind, but would find himself trapped in it until the end of his life.

# Chapter 5 - The Strange World of 1960

The late 1950s and pre-Beatlemania 1960s was a bizarre time in British culture, one which saw the rise of a variety of different cultural ideas and philosophies, almost all of which got forgotten or cast to the wayside by the Baby Boomers who came to cultural prominence in the 1960s. By 1975, the Kinks were able to sing[7] 'Where are all the angry young men now?/Barstow and Osborne, Waterhouse and Sillitoe/Where on earth did they all go?', because these once omnipresent cultural forces were now nowhere to be seen, and their influence was more or less forgotten.

Yet it was the 'Angry Young Men', and the existentialists, and the general Bohemian counterculture of the 1950s, that produced **The Strange World of Gurney Slade**. In particular, it's the peculiarly British form of the Theatre of the Absurd which intersected with the more social-realist kitchen sink drama and the new satirical comedy of the time.

Because while absurdism as a genre has a fearsome reputation as being intellectually challenging and full of theory, the fact remains that in Britain many major absurdists were working in populist genres, and in particular in comedy.

Harold Pinter, for example, was probably Britain's most prominent absurdist playwright, yet his career started in writing revue material for Kenneth Williams (who is a figure will be mentioned again later, uniting as he does several of these cultural strands) for shows that were primarily written by Peter Cook.

Indeed, the most well-known aspect of Pinter's writing, the lengthy pauses in his dialogue, stems from this period of his writing rather than from any primarily artistic motive. When writing sketches, writers are paid by the minute, and sticking a long pause in after every line of dialogue was a trick that Pinter learned in order to

---

[7] The Kinks, "Where Are They Now?" *Preservation Act 1,* 1973

make his sketches take longer to perform, and thus make more money for the same amount of writing.

Before Cook became successful with *Beyond The Fringe* (a show whose possible influence on **The Strange World of Gurney Slade** we will discuss in the essay on episode four), he was a writer for other people, and wrote a series of revues for Williams, and Pinter was a writer who was credited with additional material for these. From the perspective of 2018, Kenneth Williams, Harold Pinter, and Peter Cook seem figures who are so distinct that it's barely impossible to imagine a cultural landscape that could contain all three of them at all, yet from a 1960 perspective they were all very much aspects of the same thing. Kenneth Williams could appear in **Hancock's Half Hour** and also appear in an absurdist adaptation of *Moby Dick* with Orson Welles.

And so a lot of existentialist and absurdist ideas, in British culture, became bound up in pop culture in bizarre ways.

Many of these ideas persisted in the later sixties, as so many of the principal architects of the sixties revolution in pop culture were influenced by them, but they were no longer a major part of the cultural context the way they were from, roughly, 1954 or so to 1963. Absurdism in particular during those years was a major feature of the theatre, while existentialism had mostly taken over the kind of books that were well reviewed in broadsheet arts columns, such as William Barrett's 1958 *Irrational Man* and Colin Wilson's *The Outsider*.

But still, there was little that was pure undiluted absurdism which made its way into pop culture – absurdism had, in essence, become something which could be used as a tiny bit of flavouring in pop culture, rather than as the main ingredient. **The Strange World of Gurney Slade**, on the other hand, is as close as one can get to absolutely pure absurdism – it's more or less a perfect example of the form, especially in the latter half of the series.

While the episodes do have a vaguely plot-like structure, there's rarely anything that gives them meaning or function. There is none of what is now considered (according to the very different set of rules which are imposed by and on writers in early twenty-first century culture) to be 'good writing' – no character development, no catharses for the characters to go through. Nobody has an 'arc', and nobody goes on a Hero's Journey. Rather Gurney is adventuring through a picaresque, a series of disconnected events which just happen to follow one after the other.

Yet there's also not the narrative circularity of, say, *Waiting For Godot*. Events do resolve, episodes do have an ending, and the last episode in particular gives the whole series a neat wrapping up. This is still a series written by sitcom writers, with sitcom writers' sense of pacing, and with the awareness of the need to entertain the audience – even though, as the trailers and episode four in particular make clear, they were very aware that there was a substantial proportion of the audience who would not be entertained no matter what.

And this was typical of much of the burgeoning British counterculture at this point. Before the time Philip Larkin pinpointed in 1963 'between the end of the Chatterley ban and the Beatles' first LP'. there was a strong distinction between the popular culture of the time and the underground. 'Beatniks' were known of by the public, but viewed with suspicion. And while there was a strong stream of new artistic ideas making its way from the avant garde into popular understanding – largely because of the BBC's public service remit and lack of competitors – the people creating the art generally looked down on the popular. They often assumed the uncultured masses were incapable of understanding their work and would only like commercial pap, even as they worked to remove the boundaries between that commercial pap and their own high art.

Pop art (in its British form, which owed more to continental philosophy than the American version did) was becoming an important movement, and the popular ephemera of other eras was becoming the subject of thoughtful appreciation – in the period when rock and roll was sweeping the charts, the bohemian classes were busy listening to recreations of 1920s jazz music played by bowler-hatted Old Etonians, while the existentialists and Angry Young Men were writing works which largely consisted of encomia to themselves for their greater perceptiveness than the sheeple surrounding them.

Colin Wilson's *The Outsider*, for example, is a clear influence on **Gurney Slade** – if not directly on the series then indirectly through its influence on the culture at large. Wilson's book, intended as an examination of the figure of the outsider in literature through the ages, is more accurately described as Colin Wilson writing a book about how if you're a man who doesn't get on well with other people and reads a few books, that doesn't make you lonely and sad, no, it makes you better than everyone else.

It's also the case that in the very late 1950s, the culture was starting to become slightly more relaxed about depictions of sexuality – in particular, after the 1957 publication of the Wolfenden Report, which recommended legalising homosexuality between men (though legalisation itself took another decade after this) there was some public acknowledgement that not all sex took place between married couples, and that cultural norms did not reflect reality. The end of the *Lady Chatterley* ban, referenced above, was just one of a series of legal decisions that started to break down censorship in the UK and allow at least some of the arts to reflect something of the real world, but censorship in Britain was such that when the theatrical show *Beyond The Fringe* started, the scripts had to be submitted to the Lord Chamberlain's Office – and the stage direction 'enter two outrageous old queens' had to be edited because of the prohibition on depiction of homosexuality on the stage, to be replaced by 'enter two aesthetic young men[8]'.

The satire boom, the Profumo affair, the Beatles... all of these things, which were to cause profound liberalisation of British society, were still to come (as, perhaps most importantly, was Roy Jenkins' brief tenure as Home Secretary in the Labour government which replaced the Conservatives in 1964, in which one man did more to change British society than perhaps any other figure of the last few centuries). But the seeds of all those things were there.

---

8 Wilmut, Roger, *From Fringe to Flying Circus*, Methuen 1980, p21.

So when, for example, in episode two of the series – the episode about sexual mores – we see a fairy, wearing an Italian suit, who prefers the fairies' way of making love to the way that people like Gurney do it, who thinks fairies are 'much better than human women', and who's played by the very camp Hugh Paddick, it's not a huge leap to imagine that possibly the word 'fairy' is being used in a colloquial sense.

And a lot of **Gurney Slade** is like this when you get into the details of the series. Not that it's using euphemisms necessarily, but that it deals, in symbols and allusions, with matters that would be able to be discussed openly by the end of the decade.

**The Strange World of Gurney Slade** is, fundamentally, a transmission from another world, and another cultural context – from before the cultural revolutions of the 1960s that so fundamentally shaped the way those of us born after that time think that it's hard to imagine a time where those assumptions don't apply. But it's a transmission from the leading edge of that culture – from the part that was desperate for the changes that would build the modern world. In an odd way, precisely because of its forward-looking nature, **The Strange World of Gurney Slade** is invaluable for those of us who want to look backwards and understand that time period – even as what we see there is someone looking forward, at us.

# Chapter 6 - Episode Two

Episode two is the episode of the series which seems, in hindsight, the most of its time and the one which has least to recommend it. But this is because we live in a very different time from 1960. Attitudes towards sexuality in media from before that time can seem strange and alien to us at best, and downright revolting at worst.

Here, Gurney is exploring what looks like a disused airfield – except that in his mind and, as we later see, the minds of at least some other characters, it's actually a dance-hall. Gurney encounters a young woman (unnamed, as almost all characters in the series are) played by Anneke Wills[9], with whom Newley would shortly start a real-life relationship, but the two of them are both stifled by the conventions around dating, and so while both of them fancy each other, they both end up convinced the other is uninterested.

Gurney then decides that many of the problems surrounding love come from the way that people just end up with the boy or girl next door, rather than looking around for someone who would truly suit them. He persuades a married couple to split up and find someone better for themselves, getting lumbered himself with their children, who he provides with a new mother with the help of a fairy who is unimpressed by the whole idea of sex.

And so we have here an episode of a sitcom – never the most progressive of genres – from 1960, dealing with the subject of the relations between the genders. One might expect to find it quite appallingly cringeworthy, and indeed it is, in places.

In particular, there is surprisingly little about the conversation between Slade (named here for the first time, though still not given his first name) and the girl played by Wills which would have been different had the scene been a portrayal of an unwanted attempt at seduction rather than, as it is written, a situation in which both parties want to connect but think the other party doesn't. We know

---

[9] Wills is credited as "Annika" Wills on screen here, but Anneke is the correct spelling.

that they're both interested, because we can hear their thoughts, but play the events with only the visuals and spoken dialogue, and Slade is pestering some poor uninterested girl.

And things like the scene where Slade walks in front of a line of women to see if any of them fall in love at first sight with him, and only the coded-as-unattractive (though still perfectly reasonable looking in actuality) woman does, are somewhat less than perfect.

(Although Slade's solution to this problem – creating a copy of himself and sending the woman off with the copy – does prefigure a solution to a similar problem in an episode of **Doctor Who** from nearly fifty years later, suggesting that we have not moved on quite so much as we might think.)

However, the episode actually manages to avoid a lot of the more obvious Benny Hill-style jokes one might expect from a series whose main creative force was, after all, responsible only a few years later for writing a film with characters named Mercy Humppe, Polyester Poontang, and Filigree Fondle. In particular, it's notable that when, at Gurney's urging, Frank goes off, finds a woman he fancies, and just kisses her on the street, the response is not either for her to slap him or for her to fall in love with him, but for her to go home distraught and talk to her husband, who calls the police, who in turn drag Frank off with them, causing Gurney to re-evaluate his previous stance.

This seems, in microcosm, to recapitulate much of the sexual revolution that would happen in the later sixties, and the fallout from it which we're still seeing to this day. But it's interesting to note that nothing about the episode suggests that the treatment of Frank is unjust – it's presented as a perfectly reasonable consequence of his unreasonable actions, which is frankly a more enlightened view of sexual assault than most media presents to this day.

(This is not to say that the rest of the series is wholly free from problems around sexism, though – very far from it. Merely that the level of sexism in the series is not terrible for 1960, which is a low bar to clear.)

Everyone in episode two of **The Strange World of Gurney Slade** is straining against the rules put in their way by society, but at the same time it's accepted that those rules are sometimes actually there for a reason, and that people might get hurt more by the rules not being there. This is a rather more mature, nuanced, view of personal and sexual freedom than one might expect. This is despite the fact that the bulk of the episode is shown from the point of view of Gurney, someone who as a single man is feeling the downside of the social rules but is unaware of the worse possibilities that the rules are preventing.

Gurney's internal narration is mostly about his own entitlement to being with the women he fancies, and takes almost no account at all of the possibility that they might have a different opinion of the matter – for him, for most of the episode, the rules exist as an encumbrance, not as something to prevent real harm. It's only at the end of the episode, and seeing Frank be arrested, that he draws the conclusion that 'there's a lot to be said for this cocktail routine' and maybe sticking to cocktail parties isn't a bad idea after all.

And this is, in fact, something that we see throughout the series – everyone is straining against their societal roles, and wants to define themselves as something more than that, but finds themselves still ultimately defined by them. It's a theme that we saw from the very first scene of the first episode, when Gurney walked off the set, but still found himself at the end of the episode stuck inside a TV show, ranting at the audience to go away and leave him alone. Gurney's role is TV star, and Frank's role is married man, however much they may wish otherwise.

But there's something else we see here – an increased flexibility about the very world in which we're operating, and a blurring of the boundaries between fantasy and reality.

Whereas in the first episode everything we see is plausibly what a real person 'would' see if they were walking past Gurney at the time (though even there the nature of reality is somewhat fluid, as Gurney of course knows he's in a TV show), other than the section with Una Stubbs' vacuum-cleaner lady, episode two is more complex than that. The filming for episode two takes place, in large part, in an otherwise-deserted field, but one which is being treated by Gurney, the unnamed girl played by Wills, and others as if it were a dance hall. Are the other characters in these sequences sharing Slade's fantasy? Or are they, perhaps, part of his fantasy – but if the latter, why do we only see the people but not the dance hall?

In this respect, it's perhaps worth looking at the role of people within the series thus far. Slade's fantasies in the first episode saw him 'create' the Una Stubbs character, who we as viewers could see when not explicitly looking through the perspective of other characters – but there were characters who operated independently of Slade's fantasies, too. They couldn't see Stubbs, and their own aims and thoughts often ran counter to Slade's – Sir Geoffrey Jerome was clearly having a very different internal life from that which Slade imagined for him.

The Anneke Wills character is presented this way, rather than as a Una Stubbs style character – even though she's apparently sharing Slade's fantasy that they're in a dance hall. We hear her thoughts, and they are not the ones that Slade imagines her to have (unless he's imagining himself imagining different thoughts for her than she really has). The same also goes for the married couple that Slade discusses relationships with later – they interact with enough other people that they are clearly not figments of his imagination.

On the other hand, we also have the row of girls whose sole purpose is to fall in love with Slade (or not, as the case may be). They are clearly conjured up by Slade's imagination, as is the second Slade with whom one of them goes off. They don't interact with anyone else, and they can see the other imaginary Slade.

But then there's the problem of the children. It makes sense that they can see the fairy, if we treat the fairy as an imaginary character rather than a 'real' one – after all, they're children, and it's widely accepted that children have access to areas of the imagination that adults don't. If we take Gurney Slade as a childish or childlike figure, as someone who has access to those same areas of childhood imagination, then almost everything makes sense.

Except when he recreates their mother. This is clearly a use of his power to create people – as with Una Stubbs or the lineup of girls – but the person he creates is someone we have already seen as a real person, coded as such by the narrative.

Now, it should be pointed out here that we are not trying to assign absolute definitions of 'real' and 'imaginary' here – the narrative itself doesn't play on those terms, and doing so would be a futile effort and would be to misread everything about the series. That's especially true about this episode, all of which is, in one form or another, bemoaning the idea that we are restricted by social roles – to try to put the characters into neat little boxes would be to go against the very way in which the narrative is insisting on being read.

[It should also be pointed out that these distinctions only apply within the individual episodes – later on, characters from several different 'levels' interact in episode six, and there they all claim to be the creation of Slade himself, including several of those we have identified as 'real' here.]

But at the same time the narrative does, at times, make a real/imaginary distinction, and to go back to the matter of the field/dancehall it's made clear that what we are seeing is in some way different from Gurney's imagination, even if it is also in some ways the same. The narrative is operating on multiple levels, and it is eliding them, and at this stage of the series it's not clear to the viewer that it has a purpose in doing so.

That purpose does become apparent as the series progresses, and the series becomes more obviously an example of the techniques of the Theatre of the Absurd being applied to TV – but the Theatre of the Absurd was only in its relative infancy then, with *Waiting For Godot* having been premiered only seven years earlier, and while its ideas were part of the culture, they were very much only part of the broadsheet-reading, arts-programme-consuming, culture. This was, instead, it must be remembered, a Saturday prime-time sitcom on ITV starring a much-loved pop star and all-round family entertainer.

And so while it might be normal for a piece of Theatre of the Absurd to do all the things that **The Strange World of Gurney Slade** is doing, Newley, Hills, and Green would have all known that the vast majority of the audience will have been unaware of those techniques – and even today, the audience buying the Network DVD release is a 'cult TV' audience rather than an audience coming to the series with an expectation of something in the style of Ionesco or Beckett. Viewers today are, of course, aware of things like **The Prisoner** and **Monty Python's Flying Circus** which used some (though not all) of these ideas in a more commercial format, and so this slipping between levels of reality may seem only slightly incongruous rather than wholly so. But the viewers at the time wouldn't even have had that context to work with.

(On the other hand, of course, in some ways viewers in 1960 were more sophisticated than viewers today, in that the technological limitations of 1960 TV broadcast meant that the viewers were used to having to do more of the work themselves. It's easier to interpret an empty airfield as a dance hall if you're used to having to interpret things that are very obviously theatrical sets as dance halls, and generally having to work to interpret symbols as the things they're symbolising. TV nowadays does not deal in obvious artificiality, but always works in a mode which purports to be an accurate representation of reality.)

And in that (lack of) context, it becomes astonishing that this is the second episode of the series. Later episodes are more obviously about that slippage between reality and fiction, but they *are* later episodes, in a series which those few people still watching knew was doing something strange. Doing it here, and foregrounding it by having the very opening of the episode be filmed in a location that so obviously does not fit the action, is a brave move.

As a piece of TV, episode two is one of the weaker episodes of the series, but as a statement that this is a series that's playing by different rules, and that needs to be judged on its own terms, it really couldn't be bettered.

# Chapter 7 - On Auteurship

One factor that is important to note about **Gurney Slade** is that while Anthony Newley was undoubtedly the prime mover in the series, as its star and uncredited director (or co-director with Alan Tarrant, the producer, depending on which source you're looking at), and it fits neatly into Newley's strange sixties body of work, the actual scripts were written by Hills and Green, albeit with a lot of input from Newley.

For that reason, it's possibly useful at this point to try to distinguish their contributions, to the extent that this is possible.

Now we should note first of all that this *was* a collaboration – collaborators often find themselves creating work that no individual in the collaboration would have done, and bouncing ideas off each other until no-one is sure where an idea originated, because it doesn't originate with a single person. That is, after all, the point of collaboration in the arts. And so nothing here is to be taken as definitively saying 'this is what X brought to the table, and all examples of this are their work'.

It's frustrating, in this regard, that **The Strange World of Gurney Slade** is so ill-documented compared to other seminal TV works. Anyone who wants to can find out every possible scrap of data about the making of any individual episode of **Doctor Who**, **The Prisoner**, or **Monty Python's Flying Circus** – where every individual idea came from, who agreed or disagreed, how eventual decisions were made. In many cases it's possible (thanks to the work of dedicated researchers over a period of decades) to find every stage of an episode's development, from the first pitch to the final shooting script and beyond.

**Gurney Slade** is not like that. Other than Andrew Pixley's (excellent but short) notes for the Network DVD release and a handful of interviews conducted decades later and usually saying very little, there's really very little information out there about the series, because of the way it was more-or-less forgotten for fifty years.

In some ways, that's a good thing. We can come to the series without preconceptions as to what it was meant to be, and we can judge it without feeling like we have the creators looking over our shoulders. In some ways, we take the series as its original viewers did – as a TV series in itself, rather than as a subject for reminiscences about arguments between writers or pranks played on set.

But this does mean that there is a danger for critical analysis of hypothesising based on insufficient data, and then treating those hypotheses as established fact.

(As an example of this, I actually started an essay on the subject of whether Gurney is in fact married, based on the fact that throughout the series Newley is wearing his wedding ring, even though Gurney is portrayed as attempting to form relationships with women. Of course, this is a question that is literally unanswerable from the series itself, and the detail of the wedding ring is as likely to be a mistake or an oversight as it is a deliberate choice made by the makers of the programme. Without any way to check the authorial intention, the ring is just there, but without any obvious connection to anything else in the series the ring is also pointless).

So we have to be careful about this, but there are still some things we can establish:

Hills and Green were, first and foremost, comedy writers. Nothing else they did was at all experimental (with the possible exception of **Fancy Wanders**) but they are nonetheless the credited writers of the scripts and the presumption should be that the bulk of the actual writing came from them.

In particular, the flights of fancy and wordplay – the mandibles and countersunk screws, and the repeated jokes and catchphrases – all this almost certainly came from Hills and Green. While Newley was himself later an award-winning screenwriter, he did not have any particular aptitude for this sort of whimsy, while Hills and Green were masters of it, using it in their scripts for Morecambe and Wise and in their project straight after Gurney, **Citizen James**.

Newley, on the other hand, should be presumed to have been consulted at the ideas stage rather than to have been involved in the crafting of individual lines and scenes (though in his roles as director and performer he may well have altered things in the rehearsal stage to suit his own view of what the project should be). Looking at his own later work, the things that seem most Gurney-esque – *Stop The World, I Want To Get Off* and *Can Hieronymus Merkin Ever Forget Mercy Humppe and Find True Happiness?* – both deal with Newley-surrogate figures who are meant to represent an everyman, but who also have Newley's own particular problems with relationships (Newley was married four times and had numerous affairs), with the Newley character also being a fourth-wall breaking narrator, so we can presume that these elements were those that either came directly from Newley or at least that Newley encouraged them – the material about relationships in episode two and the love material in episode five seem the most Newley-esque in theme.

But there's also his love of metafiction – *Hieronymus Merkin* in particular plays with levels of reality and films within films commenting on the films that they're in in ways that are very Gurney-esque. We will look more at these projects of Newley's later, but for now suffice to say that these appear to have been Newley's prime contributions.

So taking all in all, it's probably safe to say that the basic thrust of the series, and certainly the things which make it most interesting to analyse, come from Newley – the climax of the last episode, the characters referencing other episodes they've watched, and the beginning with Gurney walking off the set. But the individual moments – the wishing wells and fairies, the ants and the pianos – almost certainly came from Hills and Green.

So elsewhere in this book, I will be talking about Newley as the artistic force, and to the extent there is an implied author it is him, but it is important to remember that this is, in the end, a collaborative project, not an individual one, and indeed that even in Newley's post-*Gurney* works he was usually a collaborator.

And in the book, I'll try to separate out what Newley's contribution was from Hills and Green's, but remember that this is speculative, and I could be assigning credit to the wrong people.

And wherever possible, I'll be looking at what the series does, not what the creators intended it to do. The two things may well not be the same, and it's important to distinguish.

# Chapter 8 - On Menippean Satire

One term from literary criticism which I will be using on a regular basis in this book probably needs explaining – Menippean satire.

Much of the discussion of Menippean satire was largely identified as a separate genre in the work of Mikhail Bakhtin (although Bakhtin referred to it as 'the menippea' rather than 'Menippean satire''). It takes its name from the Greek dramatist Menippus, who wrote in the third century BC and whose works are now lost, but who influenced more famous writers such as Lucian.

Menippean satire was revived in the Renaissance, and became one of the main strands of literature, though one that is often not identified as such – Menippean writing tends to straddle the border between lowbrow genre fiction (especially science fiction, though also conspiracy thrillers, mysteries, and similar) and highbrow literary writing. Its practitioners have included Jonathan Swift, Kurt Vonnegut, Douglas Adams, Dostoevsky, Jonathan Swift, William Blake, James Joyce, Lewis Carroll and Flann O'Brien.

I will be using the term as it was defined by Bakhtin, in *Problems of Dostoevsky's Poetics*. Bakhtin listed fourteen elements which I will paraphrase below, which made up the Menippean satire. As you will see, **The Strange World of Gurney Slade** fits extraordinarily well into this tradition.

Bakhtin's elements:

1. The work generally contains a lot of comedy, with a 'specifically carnival nature'.
2. It deals with the fantastical – it does not have to stick to the bounds of either realism or previously-established legend. Even when it uses legendary or historical characters, it does not have to conform to what is previously known about them. '[I]n all of world literature we could not find a genre more free than the menippea in its invention and use of the fantastic.'
3. This fantasy, however, has a purpose. Bakhtin says that 'The most important characteristic of the menippea as a genre' is that the fantastic elements are there to create an extraordinary

situation which can be used to test philosophical ideas, and that all else in the work is subordinate to that. If there's an adventure story, every element of the adventure story is there because it allows the testing of the philosophical idea under discussion. The drama in the story, if any, is driven not by character but by the truth or falsehood of a philosophical idea – a character will succeed or fail not because he (and in these works it almost always is a he, very rarely any other gender, sadly) is brave, or strong, or weak-willed, but because of his position in the world of ideas. 'In this sense one can say that the content of the menippea is the adventures of an *idea* or a *truth* in the world'.

4.  Almost as important to the genre as the testing of philosophical ideas is that the fantastic and the lofty philosophical ideas are combined with what Bakhtin referred to as a 'slum naturalism' – that the story would revel in the filth and squalor of the real world. 'The organic combination of philosophical dialogue, lofty symbol-systems, the adventure-fantastic, and slum naturalism is the outstanding characteristic of the menippea.'

5.  The philosophical questions dealt with in Menippean satire are *ultimate* questions – the questions about the nature of the universe, but also of the position of an individual (usually a man) within it. Merely academic or aesthetic questions are ignored in favour of 'an extraordinary philosophical universalism and a capacity to contemplate the world on the broadest possible scale'

6.  There tends to be a 'three-planed' construction to the narrative, with events taking place in (in the original conception) Olympus, Earth, and the nether world (or equivalents thereof in other mythical/philosophical conceptions of the universe). There are often threshold dialogues, such as arguments at the gates of Heaven.

7.  'Experimental fantasticality' – observation of normal life from an unusual viewpoint, especially from far above so it looks small, rendering it grotesque or humorous (think of the changes in size in *Gulliver's Travels* or *Alice in Wonderland*).

8. This one is perhaps the most relevant to **The Strange World of Gurney Slade**, and here rather than paraphrasing I'm going to quote some chunks verbatim: 'In the menippea there appears for the first time what might be called moral-psychological experimentation: a representation of the unusual, abnormal moral and psychic states of man - insanity of all sorts (the theme of the maniac), split personality, unrestrained daydreaming, unusual dreams, passions bordering on madness...Dreams, daydreams, insanity destroy the epic and tragic wholeness of a person and his fate: the possibilities of another person and another life are revealed in him, he loses his finalized quality and ceases to mean only one thing; he ceases to coincide with himself...This destruction of the wholeness and finalized quality of a man is facilitated by the appearance, in the menippea, of a dialogic relationship to one's own self (fraught with the possibility of split personality).'

9. Violations of normal social rules – scandals and eccentricities which 'free human behaviour from the norms and motivations that predetermine it'

10. Sharp contrasts and oxymoronic social positions – 'the virtuous hetaera', 'the emperor who becomes a slave', and so on.

11. There are often elements of utopianism, perhaps including a journey to an unknown land, or a dream, but these elements are combined with the rest of the work, rather than it being a standalone utopia.

12. That the story should have inserted elements from other genres and styles, often parodied and at a distance from the main authorial viewpoint – there might be letters or poems, or extracts from other (fictional) works.

13. The Menippean satire is multi-styled, multi-toned, and often multi-viewpoint. It's polyphonic rather than monophonic, and it assumes a view of the world in which there is not a singular truth but a range of truths which may not be compatible with each other but which are all nonetheless true.

14. The story deals to some extent with the actual topics of the day – the politics and daily lives, the events that are shaping the

culture. It may not deal with them directly, but it will comment on and satirise streams of thought and public figures that are shaping the events of the day.

And, importantly, something that Bakhtin stresses over and over when talking about these fourteen points, these things all proceed organically from each other and work with each other to create an aesthetic/philosophical whole – these elements are all working together towards a particular goal, not just coexisting.

So, looking at this list, it's immediately apparent just how many of these checklist points **The Strange World of Gurney Slade** manages to tick, despite its being a 1960s sitcom which it would at first seem inappropriate to judge by comparison to third century B.C.E. Greek plays.

Some of these points apply almost without one having to think about it. It would be very surprising, after all, if a sitcom, even an unconventional one, didn't fit Bakhtin's first point of having a lot of humour in it. But even those points which might seem less immediately appropriate often, with a little thought, can be seen to apply. The question of slum naturalism, for example, is an awkward one when dealing with something intended for prime-time ITV broadcast in the early 1960s – it was unlikely that any such series was ever going to deal with the brothels, dens of thieves, and 'erotic orgies of secret cults' that Bakhtin pointed to as characteristic of the form.

But on the other hand, Gurney *is* depicted as being unemployed and impoverished – in episode four's episode within an episode he's on the bus on the way to the labour exchange, annoyed that the bus is taking so long that the only jobs left when he gets there will be the ones where you have to work, while in episode one he steals a newspaper. He also appears to be of no fixed abode – certainly we never see any sign of him having a home (other than the TV studio he walks out of at the beginning of the series and is returned to at the end). Gurney is coded as a bohemian[10] – a word which connotes

---

[10] The term "bohemian" originated as a French slur for travelling Romany people, roughly cognate with the English "gypsy", but evolved to mean

50

about as much disreputability as primetime TV was capable of showing at that time.

Going through the rest of these points, obviously **The Strange World of Gurney Slade** deals with the fantastical, and almost as obviously it deals with ideas more than anything else. Almost every episode amounts to a discussion of different aspects of a central idea, with characters not existing as rounded characters in themselves (something that is very much lampshaded in the last episode) but as representations of different aspects of the idea under discussion.

Not all of the questions being discussed are ultimate questions, of course – there is very little of ultimate concern about countersunk screws or how an ant could carry a grand piano in its mandibles – but more than enough of them are to qualify under Bakhtin's criteria.

The main one that the series doesn't fit into is the three-planed Heaven/Hell/Earth construction, but there are multiple planes of reality here, although they often cross over rather than being cleanly separated. As for experimental fantasticality, almost all of Slade's internal monologues fall into this category, just for a start.

For Bakhtin's eighth point, we have already dealt with this in the chapter 'Is Gurney Newley?', and will pick up on this throughout the rest of the book, but it should be noted that daydreaming and multiplicity of identity are pretty much the whole of the series, in one way or another.

The ninth point, much like the fourth, has to be seen in the relative terms of what was allowed on television in the UK in the early 1960s. Mild eccentricity was allowed, even encouraged, but British TV had not yet reached the point where real violations of social norms and expectations were acceptable. Nonetheless,

---

someone who chose a life of devotion to art, poverty, and unconventional behaviour, often including comparatively few sexual inhibitions and relatively poor personal hygiene. Gurney does not exhibit most of these behaviours, but all his visible attributes belong to the kind of iconographic shorthand that was used to depict such people in fifties and early sixties media, before the bohemian was replaced first by the beatnik and then by the hippy.

Gurney's behaviour is at times certainly at the eccentric end of what was allowed, whether it be his interactions with the policeman in episode one, his persuasion of the married couple to split up in episode two, or even his walking out of the studio in the very first episode.

The tenth point is mostly absent simply by the nature of the series – without many people actually interacting with Gurney, and with those who do being simple representatives of ideas, there's not much scope for the oxymoronic. Even so, though, there are examples of this – the dog who's in charge of the farm, for example.

The eleventh item is debatable – there are certainly both journeys to unknown lands and dreams in the series, but whether one considers Gurneyland a utopia is very much open to question.

The twelfth point is very obviously true, especially in episode four, which manages to combine elements from half-a-dozen other works while also parodying and commenting on the series itself, but still true to a lesser extent in every episode of the series.

The thirteenth point is most definitely the case – and again, see earlier for more on the multifaceted and multi-viewpoint nature even of the principal character, as well as of the series itself.

And point fourteen is, again, very true – the series takes aim at everything from advertising to courtship rituals to the nature of television comedy, all in a satirical manner, and targeting a lot of what defined 1960s society.

So, what does this prove? Well, for a start, it gives us a set of criteria by which the series can be judged. The first part of any kind of artistic criticism is to identify what the work is attempting to do. Much of the discourse around fiction, in all forms, at the moment, revolves around a few ideas of what fiction is meant to be. This is not, of course, true of most serious or academic criticism, but a lot of less-serious criticism will, for example, take the rule 'show don't tell' to be axiomatic, and will dismiss voiceovers in film or an intrusive narratorial voice in prose as being examples of telling, not showing[11].

---

[11] See Kozloff, Sarah, 'Further Remarks on Showing and Telling' for examples of how this specifically affects the discourse around cinema, and causes

But this is to presume that all filmmaking, and all prose fiction, has as its sole aim the suspension of disbelief, and the immersion of the audience in a fully mimetic, 'realistic', fictional world which they can experience apparently unmediated.

This is, to put it mildly, not the aim of most Menippean satire, and it is certainly not the aim of **The Strange World of Gurney Slade**. This is a series which draws attention, at every turn, to its own fictionality and to the fact that it is a TV show, broadcast on a commercial TV network, aimed at a popular audience but not in a style which a popular audience would normally appreciate. To judge it as if it were trying to do the same kinds of things as **EastEnders** would be to apply a set of criteria which are about as appropriate as it would be to judge *Swan Lake* as a comic strip or Beethoven's Ninth Symphony as a statue.

So, if we know that the series is not intending to be mimetic, we can focus instead on what it is trying to do. This is a series which, yes, is informed by the 'kitchen-sink drama' which was just becoming popular in the late fifties and early sixties (a dramatic style which itself had far more in common with absurdism than its socially-realist reputation would suggest), but which is working in an older tradition – a tradition which, as Bakhtin points out, in fact dates back to the Classical era.

In particular, we can look at Bakhtin's first criterion – that the comedy be of a 'specifically carnival nature'. What Bakhtin meant by this is slightly different from what a plain reading would suggest, but Bakhtin was opposing it to the idea of mimetic realism in drama, and he cited in particular Bertholt Brecht and Alfred Jarry as exemplars of the carnivalesque[12]. And **The Strange World of Gurney Slade** owes

---

filmmakers to avoid a useful tool

[12] From the Introduction to Bakhtin's 'In Rabelais and His World':

"The latest development of this genre is considerably complex and contradictory. Generally speaking, two main lines of development can be traced. The first line is the modernist form (Alfred Jarry), connected in various degrees with the Romantic tradition and evolved under the influence of existentialism. The second line is the realist grotesque (Thomas Mann, Bertold Brecht, Pablo Neruda, and others). It is related to the

much to both of those playwrights, and to the absurdist traditions they instigated (Brecht was not himself an absurdist, being too concerned with the direct political relevance of his work for that, but his ideas of epic theatre, and of not causing emotional identification with characters in the audience, but instead of causing the audience to reflect critically on the artificiality of the play, were very influential on the 1950s generation of playwrights, many of whom were absurdists).

Carnival has, primarily, to do with the overthrow of an old order, and the revelation of the absurdity of social roles. In this sense, at least, **Gurney Slade** is a fully carnivalesque work. And this is something we will come back to again and again in our discussions in this book.

Because if we were to identify one overriding theme in the series, it's just this – **Gurney Slade** is an example of what happens when you reject your role in order to try to find yourself, only to discover that you were your role all along. And this is true on the macro scale of the series as a whole, and on the micro scale of every episode.

Every episode, that is, except episode three...

---

tradition of realism and folk culture and reflects  at times the direct influence of carnival forms, as in  the work of Neruda."

# Chapter 9 - Episode Three

Episode three of the series is, undoubtedly, the least essential of the series' six episodes.

Unlike the other episodes of the series, Gurney is not really the protagonist here – to the extent that there's a plot at all, he's not involved in it, just wandering around and observing the world, not really having anything happen to him other than a few conversations with other people and inanimate objects. In both previous episodes, Gurney had at least got a love interest (however flimsily characterised in episode one) to gain and lose, or some sort of problem to solve. Here, all his interactions are on a more superficial level. For that reason, there's not much necessity to recap the events of the story.

It largely consists of Gurney walking around in the countryside, including a stop by a signpost pointing in one direction to Gurney Slade, the place from which the series and its main character took its name – though the sign points in the other direction to Cuckold's Comb, which does not appear on any map which I've seen. (The theme of cuckoldry does make an appearance in the background; the wordless drama between a farmer, his wife, and a farmhand which goes on without Gurney's involvement – and which sadly features a depiction of domestic violence which would not be treated as a matter for joking these days – is one of the few moments in which someone other than Gurney takes any action this episode).

There seems to have been something of a rethink of the series after this episode, although the production dates of every episode were so close together (and so far from the transmission dates) that it can't, as one might initially imagine, be because of audience reaction. Rather there's a definite, conscious, decision made in pre-planning to have the first half of the series all take place on film, on location, and largely involve Gurney talking to himself or to imaginary characters while the second half takes place entirely in the studio and involves a lot more interaction with human beings.

To my mind, the studio-bound second half of the series is infinitely preferable to the location-based first half, but the location episodes are largely necessary, to establish a 'normal' for the series before violating that normality in the second half. However, this structural decision may well have been what doomed the series – this first half has (other than the bravura opening scene of episode one) little of the truly innovative material that makes up the second half and which is what stays in the memory after watching the whole series.

This is not to say, however, that these early episodes are lacking in merits. While they're slower and less full of ideas, even episode three contains many lovely moments of humour – the riffing on ants and grand pianos, the ongoing silent subplot about the murder of the farmer, and more – which make the episode definitely worth watching. But they're more in the vein of 'a humorous whimsical satirical look at X' rather than being the masterpieces of formal experimentation that characterise the latter half of the series. But humorous whimsical looks are still worthwhile.

Episode three is the first-half-of-series **Gurney** taken to its most extreme. There are no humans at all who interact with Gurney, other than Napoleon, and only one other humanoid character (the singing scarecrow). Gurney's story, such as it is, is carried almost entirely by Newley's voiceover and monologues – other than the farm workers' background drama, there's little here that requires a visual medium at all. Indeed, this is the only episode not to have a character reappear for the season finale, though this is perhaps understandable given the lack of humanoid involvement. But it's the one episode which could be skipped without missing anything from the larger picture of the series (other than a line about mandibles in episode six) whereas all the others have callbacks and references (sometimes in multiple episodes, as when the family from episode two reappear first in episode four and then in episode six).

Much of British TV for its first few decades was essentially televised theatre, but here we have something which is closer to televised radio, and it's here that **Gurney Slade** shows its most obvious debt to the radio comedy shows of the period – in particular the running joke about being able to carry a grand piano (a joke based on ants being able to carry so much relative to their size that it's as if a human could carry a grand piano, which slowly gets turned into Gurney believing that ants *can* carry a grand piano) is the kind of surreal repetition that had been a staple feature of British radio comedy at least since *It's That Man Again*in the 1940s, with the sheer weight of the repetition intended to turn a non sequitur into something that induces laughter.

This is a thread that most discussions of the series have ignored – there has been plenty of discussion of the obvious influences on **Monty Python** and **The Prisoner**, and some discussion of the influence that both **Hancock's Half Hour** and *The Running Jumping Standing Still Film* may have had on the series, but this thread of repetitive whimsy, which was a major thread in much  radio comedy from the 1940s right through to the 1970s, is something very few have picked up on. Wartime and post-war radio comedy in Britain was so dependent on catchphrases that listening to individual episodes of even the best series – things like **The Goon Show, I'm Sorry I'll Read That Again** or **Round The Horne** – out of context is often an exercise in confused frustration, as one is left wondering what the audience finds so hilarious about the mention of falling in the water or prunes. In more recent years this style of comedy has largely died out, with the exceptions of Reeves & Mortimer and The Mighty Boosh, both of whom are far closer to whimsical post-war comedians like Ken Dodd than is usually acknowledged.

It's an odd way to do things – the normal expectation for an early-sixties series would be that the greater visual possibilities offered by film would be taken advantage of, and that the talky, dialogue-heavy sections would be saved for the studio-bound material.

But there's an interesting way in which this *is* a visual episode, and that's the story of the three farm workers. The series, over the course of its six episodes, seems to move further and further away from Gurney engaging with 'real people' and more and more towards him engaging with only people in his imagination (although as we shall see in future episodes this boundary is blurred a lot). Here the only three human characters (other than Gurney and Napoleon) actually have a plot, more-or-less completely without interaction from Gurney. At one point Gurney puts his foot down on the farm-hand's saw, and the farm-hand lifts Gurney's foot to get it – this is the closest any of them come to interacting with each other. While Gurney is existing in his own strange world, these three are going on about their business around him, and doing so by fairly conventional rules of drama.

They're coded as being part of the real world, and we would naturally assume that they are – but are they? Even here, there's an ambiguity about what is being created by Gurney's mind and what is being observed by him. Note that we first hear of these characters' existence before we see them – from a conversation Gurney has with a dog. And they communicate entirely in mime, just like Una Stubbs' character did in the first episode. And the drama they're playing out has to do with the same themes of relationship difficulties that episode two discusses.

And then there's the fact that early on Gurney passes that sign, one direction pointing to Cuckold's Comb, and the other to Gurney Slade. The action involving the background characters does in fact take place in Cuckold's Comb, which Gurney, on seeing the sign, remarks 'obviously marks the spot of some Elizabethan shilly-shallying' – and in this case, it might be useful to note that one of the cultural idiosyncrasies of Britain in the fifties and very early sixties was a repeated reference to 'the New Elizabethans'. The idea was that the young of that time (a demographic to which Gurney Slade belonged, of course, more or less – he's meant to be in his late twenties in the series) were going to bring about the dawn of a new age much like that under Elizabeth I, and that with a fresh young monarch the country was ready to rejuvenate itself after the horrors of war. Much of the 'Swinging England' rhetoric of the 1960s dates back to this idea that the country was to be renewed by these bright young things, but the key point is that this was all tied to the figure of Elizabeth II, and that most people in Britain at the time would have considered themselves 'new Elizabethans'.

And so, what do we see in Cuckold's Comb? Cuckoldry. Elizabethan shilly-shallying. Precisely the things that Gurney thought of when seeing the place name, and precisely the sort of things that someone as obsessed with sexual relationships as Gurney proved himself in the first two episodes might be expected to imagine happening.

Or *is* it Gurney? We're back once again to the conundrum of the character's name. In this episode he does refer to himself by the surname 'Slade' in his interior monologue, but even at the end of the episode we've still never seen him refer to himself by his full name.

Indeed, on seeing the sign for Gurney Slade he says 'funny names they have in the country' – not 'that's my name!' or anything similar. Later on in the series we will see Newley explicitly playing multiple characters who look alike, but here we will just note that as well as the other oddities surrounding the character's identity, there's an unusual discrepancy between the character's spoken voice and his inner monologue, at least in this episode. When he's talking out loud to the dog, he doesn't sound like the soft-spoken Cockney we hear when he's talking to himself, but rather he sounds more like a BBC interviewer of the time, speaking in something closer to received pronunciation and politely but firmly pressing the dog on points of interest (such as what kinds of piano the dog would be able to carry) when the dog's attention wanders on to other areas of less interest to Slade (such as the untrustworthiness of the farm's hired hand).

One possible reason for this episode's comparative slightness might be that it doesn't share the themes that the rest of the series has, of breaking from constricting social roles. Whereas every other episode has characters defined by their jobs or societal expectations and breaking them, this episode deals with characters who seem happy in their roles. This is obviously true of the cow, the dog, the ant and the wishing well, none of whom seem particularly interested in doing anything differently or changing anything about their lives. The cow gets a bit bored living in the country, but still 'adores' it, and she likes the traditional milking methods used – she might wish she could get into London more often than once a year for the Agricultural Show, but she's still basically content.

Even Napoleon, in the brief fantasy sequence, fits perfectly into the *role* of Napoleon, and is content to do so – he keeps his hand in his jacket, like the paintings of Napoleon. And even Gurney, for once, seems perfectly content in the role in which he finds himself, so much so that he's 'almost tempted to stay' in the country until he witnesses the (off-screen) murder – at which point he decides to resign from humanity altogether and go to live with the ants. But where this would, in other episodes, be the start of the story, here it's the end, after spending an entire episode around characters who are happy in their roles.

This episode serves more as a breather before the relentless forward momentum of the last three episodes. As we shall see shortly...

# Chapter 10 - The Running Jumping & Standing Still Film

We'll be looking later at one possible influence on the series, with our discussion of **Hancock's Half Hour,** but there's another comedy classic from the period that may well have been a big influence on the more visual aspects of **Gurney Slade**, and especially on episode three.

*The Running Jumping & Standing Still Film* is an eleven-minute-long silent short made in 1959, starring its writers Spike Milligan, Peter Sellers, Mario Fabrizi and Richard Lester, directed by Lester, and featuring David Lodge, Bruce Lacey, Leo McKern, Norman Rossington, and Graham Stark (the latter of whom also appeared in *Gurney Slade*, as the fairy in episode six).

Many people who have commented on **Gurney Slade** have noticed the similarity between it and *A Hard Day's Night*, which Lester directed in 1964 and which also featured Rossington (Lester having been chosen in part because of the Beatles' love of *The Running Jumping & Standing Still Film*), but few have made the comparison to the earlier film. Yet, much as there are several shots in **Gurney Slade** which prefigure shots in *A Hard Day's Night*, there are also a number of elements in *The Running Jumping & Standing Still Film* which seem extremely similar to elements of **Gurney Slade**.

Some of this, of course, is a simple matter of the medium – while *The Running Jumping & Standing Still Film* is 'a film', and **The Strange World of Gurney Slade** is 'a TV series', both were actually made in the same way, using the same kind of cheap 16mm black and white film stock. And both are, effectively, shot silent – at least for much of episodes one to three of **Gurney Slade**. Those episodes have large stretches with no interaction between characters, and thus no need for synchronised sound recorded at the time – most of the sound is instead taken care of with a few sound effects and Gurney's narration.

Both were shot on location, and the field in which the Lester film is shot (and whose £5 rental cost was, according to legend, the principal expense in making the film) makes the whole thing look very like episode two of **Gurney**.

But also, there are stylistic similarities in the framing of the shots (for instance, images such as Gurney running at the end of episode three look strikingly like Lester's film). And even more than that, there's a structural similarity there. There are visual gags set up at the start of *The Running Jumping & Standing Still Film* which initially appear to be just single gags but which later recur as running themes throughout.

And episode three, with its visual background joke of the murder plot, shows that structural similarity – just as the recurring jokes, like the mandibles, are a verbal equivalent.

It's hard to say to what extent the similarities are deliberate echoes, and to what extent they're convergent evolution (and it's a shame that so little late-fifties filmed black and white TV still exists, so we can't get a better idea of how much of this was standard practice for filmed comedies of the time), but *The Running Jumping & Standing Still Film* does at least show that **Gurney Slade** was part of a movement, and a particular cinematic style. As we leave the location-shot episodes of **Gurney** behind, and head towards the more theatrical second half, we should at least acknowledge this.

# Chapter 11 - Hancock

Something that probably needs to be discussed in some detail when talking about **The Strange World of Gurney Slade** is the influence of Tony Hancock on the programme. While the similarities between the two would have been fairly obvious to viewers at the time, out of that cultural context it may be less than apparent.

In 1960, Hancock was probably the single biggest TV star in Britain. His show, **Hancock's Half Hour**, had been an immense success on the radio and later on the TV. In 1961, it would be replaced with a new series, simply called **Hancock**. Both series were written by Ray Galton and Alan Simpson, and had relatively similar formats.

While **Hancock's Half Hour** had relied on an ensemble cast – Sid James, Bill Kerr, Hattie Jacques, and Kenneth Williams – on the radio, this was cut down just to James and very occasionally Williams for the TV (and, from 1961, just Hancock as a regular cast member). This pared-down cast gave far more space to Hancock's character to talk, occasionally spending almost the entire episode expounding on his thoughts in what amounted to solo monologues. In style, rhythm, and tone, these were almost identical to the interior monologues of Gurney, although Slade's internal monologues are more whimsical and less world-weary than most of Hancock's.

As with Gurney Slade, there was a blurring of the boundary between Anthony Hancock, the performer, and Anthony Aloysius St. John Hancock, the character – Hancock the character was clearly an exaggeration of the performer's own personality traits. Both Hancocks wanted to be thought of as men who understood and cared about art and literature, men of culture and sophistication, though in the case of the Hancock of the TV programme this was a self-assessment not borne out by any evidence in the real world.

Much of the wit in **Hancock** came with the absurd, pompous, character confronting the norms of the world around him and finding ridiculousness therein, and largely monologuing about it – in the most well-known episode, for example, *The Blood Donor*, much of the time is taken up with Hancock reading out the words from posters in a doctor's waiting room, or expositing on life to a bored nurse. Similarly, *The Radio Ham*, another episode, largely consists of Hancock using an amateur radio to talk to other unseen people around the world.

These monologues are not identical to Gurney's – they're usually diegetic rather than internal monologue, and are often supposedly addressed to other people. They also tend to have a more self-pitying tone than the majority of Gurney's internal monologues (although the tone in episode two, when Gurney wishes the world would allow him a more rational way to find a girlfriend, is very close), but in rhythm and word choice they follow the monologues Galton and Simpson wrote for Hancock almost exactly.

Compare, say, this from the **Hancock** episode, *The Bed Sitter*:


HANCOCK

Not a bad set of choppers though, is it? There's a few bites left in them, but all your girlfriends have said that, don't tell a lie, all your girlfriends have said you've got lovely teeth.


Tone, they've said, Tone, you've got a lovely set of teeth. Yes, there's no sugar decay there. Which one's the bicuspid? I've been wanting to know that for years. Bicuspid. It's a funny word that, isn't it? Bicuspid. Bicus*pid*! *Bi*cuspid! By cuspid he's a handsome fellow sir Charles! [Hancock mimes fencing] Oh la, have at you sir, have at you! Bicuspid, yes, that's probably from the Latin. Bi meaning two, one on each side, cus... cuss meaning to swear. Pid... meaning pid. Greek, probably, pid, yes. Greek for teeth. Yes, so bicuspid – two swearing teeth!


with Gurney's discursion about ants and grand pianos from episode three:

## GURNEY SLADE

Look at that ant. Staggering through the grass. Must be like a jungle to him. He's carrying a bit of earth between his jaws. No, no, they don't call them jaws, what do they call them? Mandibles, that's it, mandibles.

They say that piece of earth is equivalent to a human being carrying ten times his own weight. That's like me carrying a grand piano. Just imagine what it would be like if I joined an ant colony. Lugging grand pianos about all day. Well, my mandibles wouldn't stand up to it. Down he goes into the little hole. I bet it's hell in there. Thousands of ants working like maniacs. No slacking allowed. I wouldn't last five minutes. I'd be fired for idling. The queen ant would take one look at me and give me a punch straight up the mandibles. What do they do with the idle ants? They eat them up, that's it. Any drones about and they gobble them up. It could be a very nasty business.

'Erm, Miss Pringle, send Slade in will you?'
'Yes Mr. Brown.'
'Ah, Slade, I've just been looking through your sales sheets. Haven't sold many grand pianos this month, have you?'
'No sir.'
'Been slacking on the job?'
'Yes sir.'
'Miss Pringle?'
'Yes Mr. Brown?'
'Eat Slade up.'
'Yes Mr. Brown.'
'Thank you Miss Pringle.'

There are, obviously, differences between the two pieces of writing, but there's a clear similarity in the stream-of-consciousness style, the flights of fancy disconnected from the original subject, and in the general word choice and syntax. One can easily imagine any of

Hancock's monologues during scenes in which he's bored and trying to amuse himself being placed into the mouth of Gurney, and vice versa. The differences, such as they are, come entirely from the performances, mostly due to Newley being younger and less melancholy than Hancock – Hancock's playfulness always collapses back into world-weariness, while Gurney's doesn't, at least not to the same extent.

But stylistically the two are very nearly identical. Indeed, Hills and Green clearly had a knack for writing in the Galton and Simpson style. When Tony Hancock decided he no longer wanted to work with Sid James, his foil in **Hancock's Half Hour**, Galton and Simpson created a new series, **Citizen James**, featuring James playing an almost identical role (as with **Hancock's Half Hour**, James' character was imaginatively named 'Sid James') and with Bill Kerr, who had been a mainstay of the radio version of **Hancock's Half Hour**, playing 'Billy the Kerr', another character who was essentially identical to his **HHH** persona.

This series debuted during the run of **Gurney Slade**, but after the first six-episode series, the remaining twenty-six episodes were written not by Galton and Simpson but by Hills and Green, who did a very creditable job (at least if the four surviving episodes from their run are any guide) at capturing Galton and Simpson's style, which had a much stronger level of social realism than most sitcoms of their time, and a level of emotional depth that was unusual for the period.

It may well be that Hills and Green's primary influence was precisely this – that they incorporated elements of a character who was extraordinarily popular in a medium, the sitcom, which they understood far better than Newley (who never worked on a sitcom other than this.) Certainly Newley's auctorial avatars in *Hieronymus Merkin* or *Stop The World I Want To Get Off,* while bearing some resemblance to Slade (as any character played by Newley obviously would) have a much lesser resemblance to Hancock.

Hills and Green's episodes of **Citizen James** (in which the premise was reworked almost completely from the more underworld setting of the first season to one in which James is a more amiable figure, and Kerr and Liz Fraser were dropped) stick very closely to the **Hancock's Half Hour** formula, but the resemblance to Gurney Slade can be seen very clearly in the extended riffs on mundane subjects.

For example in the second episode of season 2, *Crusty Bread* (the earliest of their four surviving episodes), there's a long argument over whether Sid's favourite confectionery is properly called a cheesecake or is just 'them shredded coconut things', and an extended discussion of the mechanics of bread-making and the different kinds of oven used, both of which bear a strong resemblance to excerpts from **Gurney Slade**, such as the counter-sunk screw episode or the discussion of ant mandibles. Indeed, this is something which is *only* in their episodes, and isn't in Galton and Simpson's more grounded first series.

Take, as an example, this dialogue from *Crusty Bread*, about the price of sugar:

CHARLIE

All the way across the Atlantic for elevenpence a pound! I'd charge a bob.

SID

You would not. You would charge one and sixpence. I know you. You don't even sell sugar, and already you're doing the public out of sevenpence just for practice.

CHARLIE

Yeah, but when you think about how they've got to refine it, and chop it up into those little square lumps, and shove it into bags... or look at it another way.

SID

I don't want to look at it another way, I'm fed up of looking at it the first way.

CHARLIE

I'm twelve stone, that's a hundred and sixty odd pound. At elevenpence a pound, that makes me about eight quid.

SID

That's about all you're worth mate.

CHARLIE

That means that I ought to be able to cross the Atlantic for about eight quid.

SID

Well if you want to chop yourself up into little square lumps and put yourself into a bag mate you're welcome to it.


The way the conversation goes from a discussion of the cost of sugar to a discussion of chopping oneself up in order to get a cheap fare across the Atlantic has much the same structure as the discussion of mandibles cited above, or as many of the other stream-of-consciousness monologues in the series.

So we see that Hills and Green doing Galton and Simpson's Hancock style gives us something very like Gurney's internal monologues, and we can tentatively say that that aspect of the series – the Hancock-esque whimsical flights of fancy from the basis of a mundane observation – is something they, rather than Newley, brought to the show.

(This is also backed up by descriptions of **Fancy Wanders**, a comedy series Green wrote twenty years later which is often compared to **Gurney Slade**. Sadly that series has never been repeated or seen a commercial release, and so I have been unable to compare it to the earlier series, but the descriptions that I have managed to read make it sound like **Citizen James** with dream sequences).

**Hancock('s Half Hour)** and **Gurney Slade** had other similarities, too – both of them touched on the same sorts of cultural references . Both series, for example, did parodies of _Twelve Angry Men_ – **Gurney Slade** in episode four by just taking a chunk of dialogue from the film and reenacting it, **Hancock's Half Hour** by parodying the plotline, with Hancock and Sid on a jury which Hancock first manages to persuade to deliver a not guilty verdict against their instincts, and then re-persuades to find the defendant guilty when he realises that if freed the defendant might burgle Hancock's own house.

Indeed, a Hills and Green episode of **Citizen James** (S3E13, *The Jury*) is all but a remake of the earlier episode, with Sid convincing the rest of the jury, all of whom were originally intending to bring a verdict of guilty, that a defendant can't be guilty of driving under the influence, as Sid knows the area and it would not be possible to crash a car into the lamppost in question, but then experimenting himself, finding it *is* possible if you're drunk enough, and reconvincing the jury to find the defendant guilty.

As well as again being a riff on the original film (which is referred to by James in dialogue), the later episode is a clear rewrite of the earlier **Hancock's Half Hour** episode, keeping several of the beats from the original, and shows the definite knowledge Hills and Green had of the earlier work.

Both **Hancock** and **Gurney Slade**, too, have a fascination with television in itself, and with the reactions of viewers to the current TV programming. And in both cases their central character is ill-defined, sometimes representing the actor who plays him and being a well-known TV star, and other times being an unemployed bohemian.

An example of the way Hancock's work resembles **The Strange World of Gurney Slade**, in content if not in form, is another collaboration with Galton and Simpson, the feature film *The Rebel*. In this, Hancock plays a variant of his normal character, who decides that he's going to walk out of his office job and pursue his dream of being an artist, despite his evident ineptitude, and moves to Paris, where he's enthusiastically accepted by the Bohemian set there, and praised for his 'infantilist' work.

The film was released only a handful of months after **The Strange World of Gurney Slade** was broadcast, and so it's exceedingly unlikely to have been influenced by it – and indeed those elements that resemble **Gurney** are almost all those which were present in Hancock's TV series – but both share a very similar theme, simultaneously mocking and celebrating the style of the Bohemians, the existentialists, and the Angry Young Men. In both cases the desire to break out of the constraints of late-fifties society is absolutely present, and is considered an entirely worthwhile thing, but is used as the source of humour nonetheless. The disaffected dreamer who wants to be a Bohemian but is, underneath, solidly lower-middle-class respectable is the centre of both works, and while Hancock's is a more melancholy work, his character was never closer to Gurney than here, at least in spirit.

But formally, the first episode of Hancock to be broadcast after **Gurney Slade** aired (the first, in fact, to be called **Hancock** and to debut the new solo format of the series) seems to be a definite response to **The Strange World of Gurney Slade**, and an attempt to go one further than its early episodes.

In this episode, *The Bed Sitter*, Hancock spends the entire episode alone, his only conversations being with people on the other end of the phone who we don't hear. The whole thing takes place within the confines of Hancock's flat, and has Hancock attempting to talk about philosophy and soliloquising to himself. It's quite apparent, watching this with the context of **Gurney Slade** having been broadcast a few months earlier, that Galton and Simpson were nodding at Hills and Green's appropriation of their style.

Indeed, there is a distinct difference in tone between the **Hancock** episodes, focusing solely on the main character, and the earlier double-act episodes of **Hancock's Half Hour**. While Hancock had decided to work without James before **Gurney Slade**, it seems likely that **The Strange World of Gurney Slade** had influenced the writers to go more in the direction that they would make their own with their later series **Steptoe and Son**. While **Steptoe and Son** returns to a double-act format, it is far more introspective, and has a far bleaker worldview, than **Hancock's Half Hour**.

Galton and Simpson's work would become steadily more influenced by absurdist theatre, especially Pinter, over the coming years, and while there had been a certain amount of that in their work from the start, one can see a *massive* stylistic change come over them immediately after **Gurney Slade** was broadcast. It seems more than plausible that they saw someone taking their ideas and running with them, and were inspired to go further themselves.

Sadly, Hancock did not go with them. After one series of **Hancock**, he moved channels (to ATV, the home of **Gurney Slade**, coincidentally) and dropped Galton and Simpson in favour of a series of lesser writers. His show never again reached the heights of his work with his original writers, and while they went on to further success with **Steptoe and Son**, Hancock's career plummeted, and he died far too young after his personal and professional lives hit rock bottom.

**Hancock's Half Hour/Hancock** never went as far in the direction of surrealism or absurdism as **The Strange World of Gurney Slade**, but the two series shared an attitude to society, and a delight in mundanity, and both were based around the ability of their central figure to hold the attention of the audience with purely verbal flights of fancy. **Gurney Slade** might have been made in some form without **Hancock's Half Hour** as an example, but it wouldn't have been in the same form, and **Hancock** in turn seems to have taken **Gurney Slade** as an inspiration to push the boundaries of its form.

# Chapter 12 - Episode Four

Episode four is where the series really starts to fulfil the potential it had shown in the first episode. Here we switch from the location-based filming of earlier episodes to studio-bound recordings, and the change is dramatic. The series goes from one based around Gurney's wandering and exploring a location, with occasional interruptions from figures on the periphery. Here, with no location to explore (and, pragmatically, with a cheap studio set rather than expensive location filming meaning that more actors with speaking roles could be hired), we turn instead to something that's much closer to the theatre of the absurd than before, and we have a totally new style of production, which owes more to Brecht and Beckett than to anything else.

Here, Gurney is put on trial, in an absurdist courtroom with no obvious rules, as he has to prove that he has a sense of humour in order to escape execution. The charge is that his series is not funny, and that in particular a monologue about countersunk screws (a monologue which we haven't seen in any previous episode, but which is very clearly in the style of those episodes) is not funny. After testimony from a typical viewing family (the family from episode two, now back together) and from an engineer who specialises in countersunk screws, the court comes to the conclusion that Gurney is not funny at all, and he is sentenced to death. However, as the axeman raises his axe, the head falls off and needs to be replaced with a countersunk screw. This is so funny that the court accepts that countersunk screws *can* be funny, and so Gurney is let off.

This is, immediately, very different from the style of the first three episodes. While those episodes were picaresques – wandering through environments, encountering characters, and hearing Gurney thinking about the week's theme as it applied to what were little more than stitched-together sketches. Here, on the other hand, there is a properly recognisable plot, with real stakes for the central character, and with other characters (the Prosecuting Counsel, the

Judge, the Executioner) who are present throughout (though other than the Prosecuting Counsel these have relatively little to do).

It's also notable that what we have here is close to a collage of elements from other works – we have fictional characters coming into the story, for example. Princess Eleanor, the judge, is acknowledged as being a character from a fairy tale – she's specifically from the old Russian fairy tale 'The Princess Who Never Laughed' (although the figure of an unlaughing Princess is a fairly common one in folk tales generally – similar figures appear in the Grimms' 'Golden Goose' (not the same story as 'The Goose That Laid the Golden Eggs') and Lang's 'The Magic Swan'). Meanwhile the barrister for the defence, dismissed early on after his inept attempts at defence by music-hall humour, referred to only by his forename Archie, is very clearly Archie Rice from John Osborne's play *The Entertainer*, which had been adapted for the screen earlier in 1960.

But we don't just have characters from different fictions appearing together. The collage elements of this story (the elements that we would call postmodernism today, but that term had not yet gained currency outside the architectural world as of 1960) extend further. The short scene with the jury starts off with an almost verbatim excerpt from *Twelve Angry Men*, except that here the 'crime' being discussed isn't whether someone committed murder but whether countersunk screws are a funny subject for comedy.[13] And we acknowledge in the story that the other episodes of the series (and presumably this one, too) are fiction – we have displayed as evidence an excerpt from another show (one we haven't seen, but which is firmly in the style of the first three episodes), and the trial for Gurney's life depends essentially on criticism of this excerpt from his show.

This is a gigantic leap forward from the whimsicality of the second and third episodes into something that's a lot more interesting formally. It's also – remarkably given that the whole thrust of the show is to deconstruct its own style – infinitely funnier

---

[13] Another possible influence for this section is the 1956 Terence Fisher film *The Last Man To Hang?*, which featured Newley in its cast and which also had a scene inspired by *Twelve Angry Men*.

and more accessible than the previous couple of episodes. While episodes two and three were paced sedately – no more so than much early-sixties TV, granted, but still slow by today's standards – episode four has a much greater rate of incident, partly because the increased cast means that there is more back-and-forth dialogue, and partly because the trial plotline adds an element of tension to the story – there are actual stakes here for Gurney, which there really haven't been in previous episodes, even if those stakes are ultimately risible. The courtroom drama gives the episode a structure, and an antagonist, two things which had been missing from the picaresques of the previous three episodes.

Of course, what we have here is still Gurney fighting against the strictures of bourgeois society – both in the person of the prosecuting counsel and in his cross-examinations of the union shop steward and the Typical TV Viewing Family (who are the first recurring characters in the series other than Gurney himself). Here the role he's trying to break free from is the role of entertainer who makes the typical viewer laugh – a role that is mocked with the inclusion of Archie the defence counsel, who exists essentially as a fifth-generation photocopy of Max Miller – but for the first time the characters here fight back and give their opinion of Gurney, so he's no longer just shadowboxing, but instead engaging in a debate.

Most interestingly, this episode would seem to owe a lot to the hit stage revue *Beyond The Fringe*, both in terms of the minimalist staging (one of the things that contemporary reviewers picked up on in *Beyond The Fringe* but which is almost forgotten nowadays, is that it made no attempt at realistic staging, using no costumes or sets other than the most minimal props, and played in front of a black backdrop) and in some of the characterisation, notably Mr Pledge, the metalworking shop steward, who seems almost identical in mannerisms to Peter Cook's E.L. Wisty. Yet this episode was filmed less than a month after *Beyond The Fringe*'s debut. Either Newley, Hills, or Green saw the show within the first few weeks of its run and quickly decided to do an episode based around its style, or they were independently coming up with many of the same ideas and concepts as that show – which, given that *Beyond The Fringe* is regularly acknowledged as one of the most innovative shows of all time, and one that completely revolutionised comedy in Britain, would be interesting in itself.

(Of course, both Wisty and Pledge are a type – in fact both of them seem to be rather unflattering caricatures of autistic people, with their flat affect, pedantic manner of speech, and obliviousness to social convention[14] – but it's a type that was not, as far as I'm aware, a regular object of mockery in British comedy prior to August 1960. (The lodger in episode one of **Gurney Slade** also seems to be an example of this type, though to a much lesser extent.) Indeed it's possible that this Wistyness was only introduced at the performance stage, as one can imagine the lines as scripted being performed in a manner more akin to Peter Sellers' Fred Kite, who was also a shop steward. It's also interesting to note that Pledge physically resembles George Reeves' version of Clark Kent from the 1950s **Adventures of Superman** TV series to a quite extraordinary degree.)

But whether there was a direct influence from *Beyond the Fringe*, or whether both were merely picking up on the same elements in the culture, it's clear that episode four of **Gurney Slade** is the first real televised example of the 'satire boom' – this is a programme that is interested in mocking its audience, and the audience's reaction to itself.

The satire boom was something that started with, and was centred around, Peter Cook and his various ventures, even though Cook himself was not really a satirist much of the time, and was more often responsible for routines like 'One Leg Too Few' (about a one-legged man auditioning for the role of Tarzan) or 'Frog and Peach' (about a restaurant that only serves dishes consisting of frogs and peaches). But between Cook's participation in *Beyond The Fringe*, his running of the Establishment Club, his ownership of *Private Eye* and

---

[14] For the avoidance of doubt, the present writer is autistic, and does not believe those stereotypes apply to all autistic people, but that doesn't mean the stereotypes don't exist.

his inspiration for David Frost, he ended up having an outsized impact on the movement. The satire boom was a short-lived phenomenon, which peaked as the Conservative government of the 1950s and early sixties headed towards its shambolic collapse, but which would, through the 1962-63 TV series **That Was The Week That Was** and its successor **The Frost Report**, end up defining much of Britain's comedy for the next few decades. If I'm right that this is an early example of its influence, this is one more way in which **Gurney Slade** was slightly ahead of its time.

And certainly Newley was to become enamoured of the satire boom, enough that in 1963 he was to record his own satirical album, *Fool Britannia*, which was written by Newley and his writing partner Leslie Bricusse, and featured Newley, Peter Sellers, and Newley's then-wife Joan Collins satirising the political scandals of the day (particularly the Profumo scandal which was responsible for the eventual end of the Conservative government), including an impersonation by Sellers of then-Prime Minister Harold Macmillan that owed a fair amount to Peter Cook's more biting version from *Beyond the Fringe*. So it seems entirely reasonable to suppose that there was an influence here.

For the first time in the series, we have other performers for Newley to work against for the whole episode, rather than occasional brief appearances in vignettes, and the programme starts to sing as a result. Gurney's confrontations with Douglas Wilmer as the prosecuting counsel are quite extraordinary, Wilmer playing the absurd situation entirely straight, as if engaging in a monologue about countersunk screws which didn't make the audience laugh was a crime truly deserving of the death penalty, and that to insinuate otherwise would be an offence against the dignity of the court. Wilmer is utterly believable in his role, and so the situation becomes at least somewhat believable.

We also have here, for the first time, the return of characters from a previous episode. The family from episode two return here, this time as a typical viewing audience – and again it shows the way the series is playing with different levels of reality that characters from one episode have watched another episode of the show and can comment on it disparagingly. Everyone in this series is aware on at least some level that they're in a TV series. There's no attempt made here to create a consistent sense of reality, or indeed to have any consistency in the characterisation – the last we saw of this family, after all, the father was being arrested after leaving his wife and sexually assaulting a stranger. Here on the other hand they are united again, and seem happy with each other (at least within the bounds of sitcom family happiness, in which a certain amount of nagging disagreement must be present).

So for the second time, counting the reappearance of the characters from the start of episode one in the scene towards the end of it, we have characters watching a series which they themselves have already been part of.

But ultimately the episode is about showing that the creators of the series had absolutely intended the reception it got. Remember that this episode was written and filmed before the first episode even aired, and yet it's entirely based around people dissecting it and missing the point, and the confusion of ordinary viewers.

There is, indeed, a certain contempt for the viewers in dialogue like:


PROSECUTOR

What did you think of the piece by the defendant?

FRANK

Well, that was clever. Very clever.


PROSECUTOR

Would you say it was funny?

FRANK

Not funny. Clever.

PROSECUTOR

Well how about you, Madam?

WOMAN

I didn't understand what it was all about. Besides, I don't think it ought to be allowed. Bad for kids.

BOY

But mum!

WOMAN

Belt up! I don't think it's good for their education. All that violence.

GIRL

Mum!

WOMAN

I said belt up!

PROSECUTOR

Thank you, Mr and Mrs Typical Viewer.

GURNEY

Mr Average Viewer, didn't you find anything in that piece funny?

FRANK

Not really... the bit about spitting was quite funny.

WOMAN

Not fit for kids to watch.

GURNEY

Oh, you found that bit funny? And how about the bit about the countersunk screw?

FRANK

What bit was that?

GURNEY

Well the whole plot revolved around countersunk screws.

FRANK

Oh. Was it funny?

GURNEY

Well that's what I'm asking you.

WOMAN

Well you can't expect us to see everything!

GURNEY

I don't know how you can miss it, it was the theme of the whole thing!

WOMAN

Well I didn't know!

This may seem like an accurate reflection of public opinion, given the drop in viewers and the number of complaints, but like all views of 'public opinion' it glosses over some rather important differences. After all. there were still five and a half million faithful viewers who kept watching **Gurney Slade** even after it was moved to its late-night time-slot and effectively disowned by the ITV network.

This is one of the few things about this episode that doesn't sit entirely well – there's an air of smug superiority here, which is calculated to make those viewers still watching think 'they don't mean *me*, they mean those sheep who have different tastes to me, unlike I, an independent free-spirited person agreeing with what the TV tells me'. This may, however, be far more obvious today in a world in which the toxicity of some people's fandom for entertainment that validates their own identities has started to have a major negative political impact.

And, to be entirely fair, this is a series saying 'only clever people will get what we're doing' *while actually doing some clever things*. It's not exactly an *Emperor's New Clothes* situation – the people it's congratulating on getting its jokes are, at least, getting jokes that are actually there, even if they're not exactly marking themselves out as part of an intellectual and cultural elite by so doing.

And that aside, this is a minor masterpiece of the televisual medium. Wilmer's performance, in particular, is outstanding, and while our hero receives a reprieve at the end of the episode, the execution scene is creepy enough that it acts as a foreshadowing of the much creepier end of the series proper.

# Chapter 13 - Fairy Tales

One thing that hasn't been mentioned much in discussion of **The Strange World of Gurney Slade** is the odd way in which fairy tales recur in one form or another throughout the series.

Episode two sees Hugh Paddick's fairy in his Italian suit — probably intended as a pun on the word as an anti-gay slur, given that Paddick himself was not only gay, but was notable for playing extremely camp characters in the radio series **Beyond Our Ken** (and in its successor **Round the Horne**, which didn't start until a few years after **Gurney Slade** ended, but is now better known than the earlier series), and the character's preference for his own mode of sexuality over human women, and the same character reappears, played by Graham Stark, in episode six.

Episode four sees the trial presided over by the Princess from a fairy-tale, identified as such, while episode five sees Gurney telling fairy stories to children, with one of the characters in his story then (sort-of) appearing.

Venturing a little further afield, there are other examples of the folk tradition here — Newley's song 'Strawberry Fair' appearing in episode five, while in episode three we not only see a magical wishing well but also get told that the nursery rhyme 'Ding Dong Bell' is a record of something that happened in the vicinity to people known to one of the characters.

Now this pattern of appearances is enough that it must be intentional — one or two mentions of fairy stories could be seen merely as coincidence, but as a thread running through the whole series it seems very different, and worth examining.

Now of course one possible — indeed likely — reason for this is that it's simply a matter of using shared cultural references, in much the same way that Napoleon appears in episode three. In the days before ubiquitous pop-culture reference points, fairy stories, folk tales, and nursery rhymes were a shared culture that could easily be used to provide a common ground for discussion, in much the same way that the style of well-known advertisements, if not their precise content, is also used in several episodes. This kind of thing can allow a writer to riff on an idea without first establishing it, and can pencil in a back story for a character – when we see the Princess in episode four, it doesn't matter necessarily if we're familiar with the particular fairy-tale she's from (and it's not one of the better-known ones), we know the *kind* of story that happens with a Princess who never laughs.

In this way she's a similar figure to the defence lawyer and the jurors – even if we've never seen *The Entertainer* or *Twelve Angry Men*, we know the kind of story that they would feature in and the kind of characters they are, and we see that elements from multiple different types of story are being juxtaposed together.

(And pastiche and collage of this type were in the cultural air at the time, with pop art making its first impact in the late fifties, with works like Richard Hamilton's 1956 'Just what is it that makes today's homes so different, so appealing?' presaging the style's wider acceptance in the sixties).

But fairy tales themselves as a genre share a great deal with **Gurney Slade**. There's often a theme of liminality, of spaces between two worlds where different rules apply. There are often characters who move between roles and identities – a King disguised as a peasant, a serving girl who becomes a Princess – and a sense that people become what they are labelled as. More generally, fairy tales are often about symbols, and the relationship between signifier and signified, so that knowing someone's name gives you power over them or an object will change its nature depending on the words used about it. They also often involve characters who are dreamers like Gurney, people who live in their own imagination but by doing so can see things that others can't.

(Of course, the corpus of fairy tales is so wide and varied that one can find any theme one wishes if selective enough, but these things do appear a great deal in many of these stories. One can speak of the fairy tale as a genre even if some examples of that genre don't fit.)

So it makes sense that for a series dealing with such themes, fairy stories would be chosen rather than, say, the story of Robin

Hood, or the tropes of the Western, which would if anything be more familiar to audiences at the time given what was popular on the TV in the period. There's a sense that in some way **The Strange World of Gurney Slade** is a fairy story, albeit a particularly unusual one. The simple-minded morality of Western stories does not really apply here, while the more complex world of the fairy story, with its ironic punishments for transgressions of nonsensical rules, seems perfectly appropriate.

Certainly episode four, in which Gurney is on trial for not being funny, and is only saved when the executioner's axe breaks and needs to be fixed with one of the countersunk screws which Gurney has been insisting are a fit subject of humour, is structured in a very fairy-story way. And episode five sees both Gurney and the Tinker as liminal figures, people who in different ways straddle the border between two very different worlds with different rules, and whose presence allows others to pass between those worlds. The only way the children and partygoers manage to pass into Gurneyland and its 'world of pure imagination' (to quote from a later Newley work) is through the assistance of Gurney.

But even in the more mundane-seeming earlier episodes, this is a world in which magic clearly exists. The world *of **Gurney Slade*** is one where our hero crosses a boundary between the real and the imaginary at the very start of the story (though in the opposite direction from how one would normally expect it to go in stories such as this – he crosses from the imaginary world of the TV series to the reality of the TV studio), and from then on the world is populated by fairies, talking dogs, sentient inanimate objects, and wishing wells.

Possibly the best comparison for **Gurney Slade**, in fact, would be Alice in Wonderland, a work which, like **Gurney Slade**, is clearly inspired by classic fairy-tales, but which uses unreal spaces and absurdity both to discuss philosophical issues and to mock contemporary society and pop culture. Of course, it's debatable whether *Alice in Wonderland* should count as a fairy tale or not, but it's hard to find a definition that would exclude it but still include, say, Hans Andersen's stories.

Using this broader idea of fairy stories, we can certainly locate some of **Gurney Slade** in that genre. Episode four, as we have seen, is very much in the tradition of *Alice*, while there's even something of the end of episode six in the climax of *Alice*, with its characters turning into playing cards.

As with much of what is notable about **Gurney Slade**, in the end it's not possible to come to a firm conclusion about the use of fairy-tale tropes and motifs in the series. Indeed, that lack of a single identifiable fixed reason for many of the decisions made *in* the series is, in itself, a big part of the appeal *of* the series.

But as we go into the last two episodes, it's worth bearing in mind that in some sense, we're watching a fairy tale. Albeit one without a happy ending...

# Chapter 14 - On the Promos

The Network DVD release of **The Strange World of Gurney Slade** contains several short promotional clips for the series, which are themselves worth looking at, as much like the series itself they seem to be playing with the form and almost defying people actually to watch the series they're ostensibly promoting.

The first couple of these show Newley dressed as Gurney, making himself a cat's cradle, while a voiceover is heard. These make a reasonable amount of sense as promotional material for the early episodes, as they display what was thought of as the selling point of the series – its similarity to the popular sketches in which Newley had appeared earlier that year.

Even these very first promos, though, presumably made to persuade people to watch a series they'd never seen before, show a quite startling amount of contempt for the prospective audience. 'They won't watch it anyway. Nobody watches television now. They just switch it on and use it as a square standard lamp.'

(These promos, incidentally, also add to the ambiguity about where the character of Gurney ends and where Anthony Newley begins, with lines like 'You might as well tell them about the social habits of Eastern Tibet. I should have done a show like that. "Anthony Newley in the Social Habits of Eastern Tibet Show"'. In these promos, Newley is definitely playing 'Anthony Newley', but he's doing so in costume, and with the characteristics of Gurney – the voiceover thoughts, and the same speech patterns.)

There's a strange kind of reverse psychology to these early promos – they are defiantly claiming that the audience won't watch it, that the programme-makers themselves were not entirely impressed with it ('I don't know what it's about and I'm in it.' and 'We should have shown them the rehearsals. We'd have been a riot.') It's as if they want to forestall all possible criticism of the show by anticipating it and using it in the publicity materials. (And one can here look at episode four, which rehearses many of these critiques in the body of the episode, as further evidence).

After these early promos, there are a set of mini promos, some only a few seconds long, which are even more bizarre. We have shots of people who aren't in the series, on a black background, over which announcers read slogans which have some connection to the series. Some of these read almost like Burma-Shave commercials (the similarity is odd given that we didn't have those commercials in the UK, but the resemblance is so strong that one wonders if perhaps they were inspired by the parodies of these ads in MAD magazine, some of which had been reprinted in the UK in 1954's *The Mad Reader*[15]) – 'Eight thirty five he's found himself a skive. He's missing his parade' or 'Eight thirty five, dig that crazy jive, he's even got a spade'. Others just play up Newley's teen idol status – a shot of a young woman looking dreamy, with the voiceover saying "Eight thirty five, and Anthony Newley!'

And finally, and most oddly, there's a promo which lasts a full minute, with Newley dressed almost as Gurney, but with a black coat rather than the light coloured one he wears in the series, stood next to a dog which resembles the sheepdog from episode three, looking at a poster for the series and talking to himself about the series in the past tense, discussing how it wasn't to the public's tastes:

> 'Well it was a noble effort, wasn't it? You tried, I'll give
> you that. You tried. But the public is no man's fool you
> know...'

There's a further clip after this which just involves Newley running back into shot, on the same set, and just looking at the poster and smiling.

Sadly, no information is given in the DVD booklet about when these clips were filmed or broadcast, which is particularly disappointing in the light of the penultimate clip, which sees Newley bemoaning the lack of success of the series. It would be very interesting to note whether this was recorded for the 1963 repeats (which seems unlikely, as it would involve getting a big star like Newley to create new promotional material for late-night repeats of an unsuccessful series, but would possibly explain the tone of the

---

[15] *The Mad Reader*, Ballantine, 1954

clip) or whether it was recorded during the original recording bloc, before the series had even been broadcast.

The latter seems more likely than it may at first appear – after all, episode four, which was recorded long before any of the series had been broadcast, can largely be read as an inquest into the series' lack of success. Clearly the show's creators anticipated much the kind of public reaction they in fact received, and so it would be entirely in keeping for them to have created a promo film based on the same kind of reaction.

There may even be some evidence as to when it was recorded. A message board post at the Cook'd and Bomb'd website[16] has a (sadly unsourced) list of studio recording dates for the series. It has no studio date for episode two, as that episode was shot entirely on location, but does have one for episode three, which is also entirely on location. It would be reasonable to assume, absent better evidence, that the promo in question (and the short follow-up one on the same set) was filmed during that studio slot.

This would also explain the oddity of the poster on the wall advertising the show, which both Newley and the dog are looking at, having a time of 7:30 even though (as the voiceovers in the earlier promos make clear) the earliest any episode of the series was broadcast was 8:35.[17] If it was filmed, as I suspect, on the 16th of September 1960, a good six weeks before any of the series was actually broadcast, it would be reasonable to imagine that the original plan was for the series to be broadcast at 7:30, and that this plan was changed at some point in the intervening time.

(Annoyingly, Newley's left hand is out of shot at all times in these promos. This could have settled the question definitively, as Newley did not wear a wedding ring during his marriage to Joan Collins, who he married in May 1963, but did during the filming of **Gurney Slade**, in the middle of his previous marriage.)

---

[16] 'Re: The Strange World of Gurney Slade'.
[17] Although it could also be argued that if this was filmed in 1963, the makers may simply not have remembered what time it was shown originally.

If I'm correct, the tone of the promo is quite astonishingly bleak given that no-one knew what the series' reception was going to be at the time of filming. Newley, talking to the poster of Gurney Slade, says 'The public knows what it wants. And you had no right to even try and suggest something different' and goes on to mock public tastes, dismissing then-popular series like **Wagon Train**, and being simultaneously contemptuous of the public for the dullness of their taste and of Gurney (here portrayed as the instigator of the show) for thinking that the general public could ever be convinced to watch anything of merit. Newley himself is portrayed as a cynical, mercenary, figure, whose only desire is to have an easy life and get paid.

It's quite possibly the most profoundly bleak piece of advertising ever made, and it can't possibly have been expected actually to persuade anyone to watch the series it was advertising. Like episode four, it may have reassured those who were already watching (or who had previously watched) that they had more sophisticated tastes than the public as a whole, but it wasn't going to entice anyone to become a new viewer.

As a whole, these promo videos add to our understanding of **Gurney Slade**. Even discounting the long elegaic one, they show that the programme-makers were already convinced of the likely failure of the show with the viewing public. But they also have a defiance to them that is almost (to use a critical cliché) punk rock. There's a bravado here, a sense of sticking two fingers up to the audience and saying 'damn you, we didn't make this for you', which is somewhat jaw-dropping despite everything.

# Chapter 15 - Episode Five

Episode five once again starts us looking at the borders between imagination and reality which have proved so porous previously.

We start with Gurney reading a story to a group of children, who are eager to see the magic Tinker in the story, who they believe is real. Gurney starts to teach them about the power of the imagination, and says that the Tinker comes from Gurneyland, a land you can see if you close your eyes. A young couple, Albert and Veronica, arrive, and Gurney persuades them to imagine Veronica as more beautiful than she is, inadvertently destroying Veronica's attraction to Albert even as he increases Albert's attraction to Veronica. Then an actual tinker arrives, and is bemused by the children's insistence that he do magic for them, before they all decamp into Gurneyland, inside Gurney's mind, for the altogether stranger second half, including a guest performance of Anthony Newley's latest hit single, by a singer who looks a lot like Gurney.

Here we finally get to the logical consequence of the positions we set out in episode one, that characters and situations from Gurney's imagination can interact with and change characters who Gurney has not created (although again, if episode six is to be believed, Albert is the creation of Gurney as much as anyone else is, even though he later journeys into Gurneyland).

Here in fact we see all the themes start to come together before the big finale. We have the themes of sexuality and the difficulty of communication between prospective sexual partners as Albert and Veronica try and fail to get together. We have the multiplicity of Gurney/Newleys coming to the forefront, as we have the 'real' Gurney, the devilish Gurney, Gurney's depression, and the singer who might or might not be Gurney but who is performing a contemporaneous hit of Newley's. We have the examination of Gurney's mind, which has previously been done as monologue, now given form as an actual exploration of his mental landscape, so tying those earlier monologues to the more general style of exploration we have seen. And we have once again the implication that the characters in the series are able to watch the series on TV, as when Gurney asks the children to whom he is telling his stories if they want to watch TV instead, they reply that the only thing that's on is some bloke telling kids stories.

The oddest thing about this episode, though, is the way it gives a characterisation to Gurney, and one that is quite at odds with the way he's portrayed in other episodes. Partly this is because here Gurney has to be opposed by his own devilish impulses, and as such he has to be portrayed as more purely 'good' than he was previously. So where in previous episodes Gurney has seemed to be driven mostly by curiosity, with a slight admixture of sexual interest in women, here he's a little bit of a prude – he takes great offence at the idea that he could be interested in watching a pornographic film, and he's interested in preventing himself from having a dirty mind. He's also the kind of person who happily tells fairy stories to gangs of eager children, which also does not really seem to be in keeping with the characterisation in the rest of the series.

This straight-lacedness, though, contrasts with his behaviour towards Albert, who he encourages to be more of a 'raver', and in those conversations he seems convinced that the main problem with society is that it is too inhibited, which doesn't appear to sit well with the rest of his characterisation (but which, interestingly, would sit entirely fine with Gurney's inner devil). It's a tribute to Newley's consistency in his performance that he manages to convince as the same character throughout.

What's interesting to note here is the way that Newley modulates his performance. While Gurney himself is played as very straight-laced (again, more so than in previous episodes, where he's seemed almost flirty when, for example, talking with the cow in episode three), he seems more self-conscious about how people perceive him here. By contrast, Gurney's devilish side is flamboyant (and, frankly, camp, though a weirdly heterosexual sort of camp – there's thankfully no overt connection between homosexuality and evil made here), with almost every syllable spoken a chance for a new facial expression more extreme than the last.

The devilish side of Gurney's character is also more than happy to use beatnik slang, in a way that Gurney simply doesn't – the language used is completely different, and suggests that as much as anything he's Gurney's inner hipster. In many ways, though no-one involved could have known that, Gurney's inner devil might almost be an incarnation of the spirit of the 1960s, with his hip language and his advocacy of sexual freedoms.

And the devil is of course not the only other character Newley plays here – we have what may be read as the first intrusion of 'Anthony Newley' as a character in the series, with the performance of 'Strawberry Fair' (though with notably different lyrics in parts to his hit single version). 'Strawberry Fair' was a traditional folk song, but the version of it performed by Newley has its lyrics largely rewritten by one 'Nolly Clapton' – a pseudonym for Newley himself. The song itself perhaps seems more appropriate for episode two, as even in the bowdlerised version by which it's known today (the song was collected by the noted folk song collector the Rev Sabine Baring-Gould, who is best known for writing 'Onward Christian Soldiers', and who edited the lyrics of the songs he collected to make them more suitable) its innuendos about a young woman asking for her cherries to be picked would have more relevance to that episode's discussion of sexual mores.

(Although that said, both the folk song and the fairy tale come from similar traditions, and so it is perhaps fitting that in an episode where Gurney Slade is telling fairy stories to the children one has a folk song about refusing the food offered by a stranger.)

We don't know for sure who this other Newley character is – it could be read either as Gurney himself (since he says at the end 'I should have thought that would have driven them out. Funny, I always had the impression I sang better than that') or as Newley (since it is, after all, Newley's hit single, and we know that Newley later turns up as a character himself), or as some deliberate blurring of the lines between the two.

Not only that, but there is a *fourth* character played by Newley here, Gurney's depression, a figure that exists in an altogether more unpleasant state than Gurney or his devilish side. In a series which slyly implies a multiplicity to its main character (or characters) this is an episode which, more than any other, tells us that there is not one Gurney Slade but a mass of them – and indeed the implication that Gurneyland can be in anyone's mind implies that we are all, all of us, Gurney Slade in a way, even as the series is about a specific iteration or iterations of the character.

But this also introduces the idea that there *is* a darkness to Gurney's nature, something we hadn't seen before, other than his brief railing against the audience at the end of episode one (and, arguably, his sullen refusal to participate in the sitcom at the start of episode one). Up to this point, to the extent Gurney has been characterised at all, other than just as an everyman, it's been as something of a tricksterish figure, one who messes things up to see what happens, but with no real darkness to him. Now we see his devilishness and his depression for the first time, turning him into a far more rounded character, right before the last episode which is going to rely on us identifying with Gurney himself as a character (even as it points out his artificiality).

All of these performances rely for their differentiation on body language – Gurney is, as always, essentially a neutral figure, with inexpressive body language, but his devilish side is a mass of movement in his face, while his body language is simultaneously relaxed but suggesting a tension that would allow him to pounce at any minute. Gurney's depression is hunched over and small, while Newley-the-singer is giving a standard pop performance of the time. All four would be recognisable from silhouette alone, which given that they're played by the same man is an achievement.

And this points to something worth noting about this episode – it's the only one to make full use of the visual possibilities of TV (at least, again, other than the last few minutes of episode six). While the first three episodes are shot on location in real places, and episodes four and six are shot in the studio but in front of largely black, minimalist, backdrops, this episode has a variety of sets which work hugely evocatively – the sets inside Gurneyland make no attempt at realism, looking more like the backdrops from late-1950s cartoons, but they set out a space which we explore, rather than, as in episode four, a void in which the characters hang (or episode six in which they are all only present in a completely undisguised TV studio ). In an episode where we're told over and over again that we can imagine things that are more fantastical than we can see with our own eyes (and indeed we are shown this with the Tinker's production of ever more ludicrous imaginary objects), we still have, for the only time, an attempt to represent the visual imagination in the picture.

For all that TV is a visual medium, TV in Britain in the 1960s was a medium that was largely an outgrowth of radio and theatre, two media which are based far more on the spoken word than on the image (which is one reason why it's such fertile ground for criticism, and why British TV of the classic era tends to have so much more written about it than its American counterpart, which grew out of cinema and so emphasises visual spectacle rather than verbal skill).

But here we have the set designers set loose to create a physical world that represents Gurney's internal state, and what we have is something quite marvellous, with everything working as flats, walls that you can see round and which are clearly no barrier, solid objects reduced to drawings on the walls – everything is not only unreal, but very obviously unreal, and it again fits with the overall threads of the series – the obsessions with breaking down borders, and with things not being themselves but instead being representations of themselves.

In all, episode five takes all the elements of episode four – the metatextuality and metafictionality, the obsession with the programme itself, the complete change in visual style from the first three episodes – and amps them up several notches. After seeming to run in place somewhat with episodes two and three, the series now has a clear momentum. It's going somewhere, and when it reaches its destination in the next episode, we'll see that it was going somewhere quite special.

# Chapter 16 - The Music of Gurney Slade

It's probably worth devoting some small amount of time to a discussion of the music in the series, since not only was its star himself a pop star and songwriter, but the series' theme tune is by far the most widely known aspect of the show.

The theme tune, by Max Harris, is now far better known (at least among the generation currently in their forties and fifties) as the music used in the animated clock sequences of the popular children's programme *Vision On*, which ran from 1964 to 1976. Even before this use, the tune was so popular that it managed to reach number eleven in the singles chart – a singular achievement for the instrumental theme tune to an unpopular TV show. Harris was, by inclination, a jazz musician, though he made most of his money in TV work, and the **Gurney Slade** theme is definitely influenced by contemporary jazz – it resembles nothing so much, in fact, as the music that Vince Guraldi wrote for *A Charlie Brown Christmas*, although there's also an element of Dave Brubeck in there.

Harris composed all the music for the series, and it was performed by ATV's standard set of session musicians, led by Jack Parnell. Parnell, whose uncle Val Parnell was the managing director of ATV, conducted the ATV band from 1957 to 1981, playing on everything from **Sunday Night At The London Palladium** to **The Muppet Show**, but while he got the role through his family connections, it was certainly not pure nepotism – he had been a serious jazz musician, whose band had contained figures such as Ronnie Scott and Tubby Hayes, before going into TV work, and his jazz sympathies can definitely be heard in the music here.

While we have argued that **The Strange World of Gurney Slade** is not really a sitcom, one of the ways in which it does resemble the sitcom genre is in the use of music. Music is used only sparely in the series, and that use is front-loaded in the first two episodes, with the silent-movie sequence involving Una Stubbs' advertisement character, and the 'dance hall' sequences involving Anneke Wills, making up the majority of its use.

Apart from these occasions, to point up that the silent-movie section *was* a silent-movie section in the first case, and as semi-diegetic music in the second, music generally performs the same function in the series as, say, Angela Morley's scores for *Hancock*, in which music is mostly used for transition between scenes, to underscore what might be seen as punchlines, or over dialogue-free linking sequences. This contrasts with the way in which music would be used in more dramatic productions, where it would be used more to guide the viewers' emotional reactions.

This should probably not be overemphasised – British TV in the late fifties and very early sixties used very little musical score in comparison to current TV, largely because of the technical issues involved in doing so when most TV was performed as live. But to the extent that one can differentiate between sitcom and drama music usage, **Gurney Slade** falls firmly on the sitcom side of the line.

The theme music is, of course, also the first sign that there is a blurring of the diegetic and the extra-diegetic going on in this series, when in episode one, as Gurney walks off, he starts to play air piano to the theme tune. He does this several times in the series, all at times which in a more normal show would be considered moments of fourth-wall breaking (in this series, not only is the fourth wall comprehensively shattered, but so are several other walls we would not even have considered walls). So while the use of music in the series is minimal, it's absolutely important nonetheless.

The other obvious piece of music to discuss, and indeed the other hit single connected with the series, is 'Strawberry Fair', which Newley performs in episode five, and which had been a hit for him a short time previously.

Newley's pop stardom was comparatively short, but hugely influential – the obvious influence that everyone talks about is on David Bowie, who in his early years sounded, frankly, like an Anthony Newley tribute act, and who even later on owed a *lot* to Newley's vocal style, but it's also very possible to see his influence in mid-period Kinks records such as 'Autumn Almanac', and in the vocal style of Steve Marriott, especially around the time of the Small Faces' *Ogden's Nut Gone Flake* album, which was the height of Marriott's use of his natural Cockney accent on his records. One must also not forget Davy Jones of the Monkees, whose accent in his performances sounds more like Newley's than Jones' own native Mancunian, and who used to cover Newley's 'Gonna Build A Mountain' in his stage shows (Newley and Jones both made their names playing the Artful Dodger – Newley in David Lean's film version of *Oliver Twist*, Jones in the West End production of *Oliver!* – and Jones seems to have emulated Newley's performance style deliberately).

The odd thing about this is that Newley's music, while it influenced a whole generation of extremely progressive musicians, has almost no connection to the rock music they otherwise loved, and this is very obvious on 'Strawberry Fair'. This is a performance of a traditional folk song, but with lyrics rewritten by Newley. There's absolutely no rock influence in his vocal, which is casual, and owes more to the laid-back style of crooners such as Tony Bennett than to the more overtly emotive and passionate vocals of the rock era (though it's possible to overstate the implications of this – remember that in the pre-Beatles 60s, the biggest rock and roll stars in Britain were Cliff Richard and Tommy Steele, neither of them particularly known for their howling passion), while the backing uses rock instrumentation such as electric guitars, but in a manner that owes nothing to the blues-inflected tonalities of rock music (it owes a great deal, however, to the experimental hit singles produced by Joe Meek, which often combined similarly incongruous elements and which also often had the swimmy, thin, instrumental sound that Newley's single had).

In its own way, 'Strawberry Fair' heard now seems as strange as **Gurney Slade** itself does. While it made perfect sense in the context of the charts of 1960, where it jostled with Roy Orbison, The Drifters, and Elvis Presley, but also with the guitar instrumentals of Bert Weedon and Johnny & The Hurricanes, the novelty records of Charlie Drake and Peter Sellers, and Adam Faith singing about lonely puppies and Frank Sinatra singing a swing version of 'Old MacDonald's Farm', the accepted cultural history of pop music has erased almost all these disparate strands of music from the collective memory, and 'Strawberry Fair' sounds like a broadcast from an alternate universe where the Beatles never happened and rock music was merely a late-50s fad.

While **Gurney Slade** was so far ahead of its time that it still looks fresh, 'Strawberry Fair' was so much of its time that it seems incomprehensible that it could even exist.

But this is something we have to bear in mind while examining the series as a whole. **The Strange World of Gurney Slade** is, after all, a message from another world – a world where people still in their thirties had fought in the Second World War, where Britain still had an Empire, where there were only two TV channels, and where nobody outside of Liverpool had heard of the Beatles. While some of the series seems strange and fascinating to us because it was genuinely innovative, other aspects will seem almost as odd just because they are based on a set of assumptions about the world that are now almost completely incomprehensible to anyone under sixty (and indeed which many over that age will find alien now – one finds all too often that one projects the current cultural context back in time, and it's easy to underestimate the profound shifts that can take place in a matter of a decade or so, let alone nearly six decades).

So the oddness of the music here is a useful reminder when discussing the series as a whole – what we may take, as viewers outside that context, with a limited amount of information about early-60s TV, as being wildly innovative, may equally be a norm from the time which we have now lost.

But this does not mean that it has less value – part of the interest in old works of art is to see the potential roads that could have been taken but haven't been. It's just a distinction we need to make, and so having 'Strawberry Fair' in the series is a useful reminder that the past really was a different country, and that much like in Gurneyland they did things very differently there.

# Chapter 17 - Episode Six

Episode six of **The Strange World of Gurney Slade** is the ultimate culmination of everything that the series was leading to from the start – an explicit acknowledgement within the text of its own fictionality, with characters from every episode (except, notably, the third episode) reappearing and challenging Gurney as their creator.

We start with a clueless businessman or politician type being shown round the studio, with Gurney sitting silently as the boom mic, the cameras, and the performer are explained to the businessman in similar terms, before the show proper starts. As Gurney reminisces about how this studio was where he was born a few weeks earlier, we keep cutting to the control room, where the hand and voice of the director can magically override Gurney's own will, and where there's a countdown to the end of the show. Characters from previous episodes appear, and demand that Gurney provide them with back-stories and characteristics they were missing in their earlier appearances, but he can't as there simply isn't the time any more.

Eventually a compromise is reached, and the characters go on to appearances in new books and TV series (with moments of pathos like the couple from episodes two and four being separated from each other and their children) before the final end, where Gurney is alone and confronted by his creator – Anthony Newley – who listens impassively as Gurney begs for his life. Gurney slowly turns into a ventriloquist's dummy before our eyes, even as he continues begging, but to no avail. The last shot shows Newley carrying Gurney, now just an immobile dummy, out of the door through which Gurney had originally exited to freedom six episodes earlier.

The episode is clearly inspired by Pirandello's early absurdist work *Six Characters in Search of an Author* – or at least by depictions of that work in popular culture. For very obvious reasons it doesn't touch on any of the many disturbing themes of that work – incest, sex work, and family breakdown[18] – concentrating solely on the metafictional element of characters who are 'incomplete' and need an author to complete their stories.

But the episode also reveals the nested metafictionality of the series – all the characters are aware of their status as creations, but refer to Gurney as their creator. But it's specifically Gurney – the fictional character who exists in the same fictional world as them – who they regard as their author (and that's the word used, even though they're televisual characters rather than literary ones). Yet the fact that Gurney himself is also fictional is made very clear from the beginning – as is the fact that he exists in a specific commercial/cultural space, as a very specific product of early-60s commercial television.

From the moment the episode opens – in the same TV studio where the first episode started, with Gurney motionless as he's inspected by people who are coded as being of some importance but who have no idea what the company even does, or such basics as what a camera or a performer are – we're being told that this episode is about TV itself, and specifically about commercial TV and the cultural factors that go into producing it.

Obviously all the way through the series we've seen advertising play a role – whether in the poster in episode one, the discussion of the countersunk screw advertising in episode four, or even the way that the promos for the series play with the form (and indeed the later ones feature Gurney looking at an advertising poster for the show itself), but here we see the culmination of this, even though advertising itself is barely referenced in the episode. The programme we're watching is the product of commercial imperatives, and the

---

[18] With one exception. The nameless character played by Anneke Wills finds herself, at the end, sent off to appear in "one of those French films", in which she will have to appear nude, and when she's told that it's not important because her mother will never see it, replies "Daddy will though – he goes to Paris on business!". This bears enough resemblance to Pirandello's theme of unknowing father/daughter incest and sex work that the reference is surely deliberate, although toned down enough to, just about, pass muster by early sixties TV standards.

- people making the ultimate decisions about it have no more idea of how TV is made than they do about anything else.

(Though, again, we should point out that we're playing with multiple levels of reality here, too. After all, the characters we're seeing are just that – characters in the series. No matter how metatextual the series gets, and no matter how many levels of awareness of its own fictionality the characters show, at the end of it all they are still characters rather than real people, and they still exist within the TV show and are unable to escape it.)

Everything comes together here, as we see that the show we're watching is the product of cultural and commercial decisions, and of the reality of TV making. A director hovers over the whole proceedings, seen only as a disembodied hand working the controls and heard as a voice giving orders which are immediately obeyed by the characters, despite their own objections, as if he's an interventionist God able to override free will. (And the fact that there is no credited director on any of the programmes adds to the mystique here. It's widely reported[19] that Newley himself was either the *de facto* director or co-directed with producer Alan Tarrant – another data point in the discussion of who was ultimately responsible for this – but he's never credited as such). But even that interventionist God himself is overridden by further external factors – he has to keep account of how much time they have left in the studio, and when to break for commercials. And, of course, even the interventionist God exists in the fictional space, not the real one – no matter how close the series gets to realism, and here it looks as much like a documentary about the making of a TV series as it does an absurdist play, at least at times, it's still a scripted series. We see the characters, we see Gurney as the inventor of the characters, we see Newley as Gurney's inventor, we see the director who gives Newley his cue, but we never see the ultimate level of creation. Indeed, it's not possible for us ever to see the ultimate level of creation.

---

[19] For example at
https://www.clivebanks.co.uk/Gurney%20Slade%20Intro.htm and
https://letterboxd.com/film/the-strange-world-of-gurney-slade/crew/

(Although it's also interesting to note here that each level is a little more mundane than the one before. Gurney's creations include fairies and Queens, while Gurney himself is, other than his powers of imagination, a fairly normal person, and Newley himself of course existed in the real world. There is, at least implicitly if never explicitly, a link made here that suggests something of Platonism, ideal forms being more beautiful than their echoes in reality. Of course, Platonism is a recurring element in British fantasy fiction and telefantasy throughout the early and middle decades of the twentieth century, so it's unsurprising to see it here, in what is the most philosophical of all TV fantasy shows, if indeed that's how we choose to categorise this series).

Every character here is conscious of their ultimate fate, and trying desperately to escape it. They all know that when the series ends they will cease to exist, and furthermore that their existence is only sketched in the broadest of strokes – a pretty young woman, a prosecuting counsel, an executioner – none of them aware of having a personality or attributes outside those needed for their earlier brief scenes.

It's here that we realise that **Gurney Slade** has, all along, been about escape from roles, but when your social role is all that you have, what 'you' is there to escape it? Eventually, there are happy endings for the various characters, all of whom are generic enough that they can be reused in other series and books, whether that be **Emergency Ward 10**, Enid Blyton's next book, or a pornographic film. And indeed it would be nice to imagine the characters all continuing to have lives throughout the different works they appear in, accreting a little more character with each appearance as 'man on street' or 'girl in shop' throughout decades or centuries, slowly becoming the fully-rounded characters they always wanted to be.

But Gurney is a different matter. Because he's stepped fully out of his role, he no longer has one. He can't be repurposed for a role in **Boyd QC**, because he's too specific to be generic, so when the context for which he was created ceases to exist, so must he. It's all, once again, about contexts. Gurney Slade only makes sense in the context of a single TV series, and without that context – even though, from the very beginning, he's wanted to escape it – he has no characteristics that separate him from the actor Anthony Newley. In the end he's not a real boy, he's just a dummy, and everything about him that gives him life walks away in Newley's body.

This is the ultimate horror of the series, as we see Gurney begging for his existence even as he slowly turns into a ventriloquist's dummy, in one of the most existentially terrifying moments of the series. Throughout the series, Gurney has wanted to be free from social roles, and has urged others to just be themselves, from walking off the set in the very first episode, through his attempts to make Frank leave his wife and find someone better for him in the second, right through to now. But he has discovered that there is no real him to be. He is, himself, just another role to be discarded by an actor. When you strip away the relations with the rest of society, when you go exploring deep inside your own mind, what you find at the end is that there is nothing left to be.

Many fans of cult TV have pointed out the similarities between the last episode of **Gurney Slade** and the more famous, later, last episode of **The Prisoner**, and the two series have many parallels – both were made by ATV (**Gurney Slade** directly, **The Prisoner** through the wholly-owned subsidiary ITC), both had similar themes of trying to break out from roles assigned by others, and both were the work of auteurish performer/directors (although Patrick McGoohan did far more of the actual writing for **The Prisoner** – though he is similarly sometimes overcredited as the only important creative voice in the series, just as Newley is for **Gurney Slade**). Indeed it's possible that McGoohan gave a sly nod to Newley as an inspiration in the later series – 'Pop Goes The Weasel' is a regular musical leitmotif throughout the series, and Newley had a hit with his own idiosyncratic take on the children's song in 1961.

But while both series have a similar climax – in **The Prisoner**, Number Six (the protagonist) confronts Number One (the ultimate villain of the series, whose identity has been set up as a big mystery since the first episode), who removes several faces which are revealed to be masks before eventually showing Number Six's own face, while in **Gurney Slade**, Gurney comes face to face with the actor who plays him and his own true nature – **Gurney**'s is far, far, more unnerving. In **The Prisoner**, the implication is that you are the author of your own misfortunes – it's fundamentally a solipsistic worldview, in which only Number One exists. In **Gurney**, though, things are far more nihilistic – even Gurney Slade himself doesn't exist. We're all just puppets of uninterested gods, who are themselves puppets of larger forces. If you try to find out who you are as an individual, to escape your social role, and to exercise free will, you'll find that you can't – larger forces are arrayed against you, and even if they weren't there's no 'you' to do the escaping.

And this is something promoted as a sitcom.

The ending of the series is profoundly bleak, and makes it very clear that the programme-makers saw no possibility of the series being revived, even though it was filmed before the series was broadcast at all. The whole series becomes, in retrospect, about fighting battles that one can't possibly win – with the TV company, with the viewers, and with oneself – and the message is, ultimately, 'don't try anything new. Trying to change things will kill you.'

I'm sure Gurney would have liked to have said goodnight, and to thank you for watching. Goodnight.

103

# Chapter 18 - Post-Gurney Works

When looking at **The Strange World of Gurney Slade**, one should be aware that it is fairly early in its creators' careers. In this section, we're going to look briefly at some of the other, later, works from the series' creators which might shed light on the series.

Much of what both Newley and the Hills/Green team did post-**Gurney Slade** was rather more in the mainstream of light entertainment than **Slade** itself had been. Hills and Green were best known for their work for Morecambe and Wise in the 1960s, where they developed many of the running gags and catchphrases that sustained the act for the rest of their careers (Hills and Green were replaced by Eddie Braben when Morecambe and Wise transferred TV stations, and it's Braben's work with them that's best known, but examination of the surviving material Hills and Green wrote for the duo shows that much of what they're known for was already in place then). Newley, meanwhile, had a career that spanned regular appearances on **Hollywood Square**s, writing the songs for Willie Wonka and the Chocolate Factory, and, shortly before his death, a regular role in the soap opera **EastEnders**.

But even so, there were still signs in some of their later work of the experimentation that led to **The Strange World of Gurney Slade**.

## Stop The World, I Want To Get Off

One of Newley's most successful projects, this stage musical began in 1961, shortly after **The Strange World of Gurney Slade** ended, and was very similar to the earlier series thematically. However, while **Gurney Slade** had been a comparative commercial failure, *Stop The World I Want To Get Off* was a massive success.

Written by Newley with his songwriting partner Leslie Bricusse, and starring and directed by Newley, it ran for 485 performances in the West End, transferred to Broadway where it ran for a further 555 performances (also initially directed by and starring Newley), and was filmed twice (a film version in 1966 and a TV movie version in

1996), spinning off the successful songs 'Gonna Build A Mountain' and 'What Kind of Fool Am I?'

The play tells the life, from birth to death – and rebirth – of an everyman character called Littlechap, who gains success by marrying his boss's daughter, and then goes on to have affairs with various women who represent national stereotypes (all of whom were, at least in the original production, played by the same actor who played his wife, and thus readable as different facets of an everywoman), before eventually realising that he loved his wife all along. The play ends with Littlechap persuading Death to take him, instead of his newborn grandson, and then being reborn to restart the cycle of birth, sex, and death, much as the world itself continues to turn.

Littlechap's frequent interjections of 'stop the world!', followed by fourth-wall-breaking soliloquies to the audience, any time his life doesn't go as he wishes, show that Newley was continuing to think about the possibilities of characters knowing they're part of a text, and the musings on sexuality and relationships owe a lot to the second episode of *Gurney*, while the ending (cut from the film adaptation) is slightly more upbeat than that of **Gurney Slade** (what isn't?) but is definitely of a piece with it.

## The Small World of Sammy Lee

This 1963 British noir film has little to do with **Gurney Slade** in itself, but given the similarity in the title (no doubt deliberate – it was based on a TV play from 1958, which Newley had also starred in, which was simply titled 'Sammy') and the fact that Newley (who starred) wore an outfit that was similar to that which he wore in the series (other than the substitution of a bow tie for the more normal tie Gurney wears, as Sammy is a nightclub entertainer), it's worth at least a brief mention here.

(The similarity in names is probably what led Eric Idle, for example, to talk about being influenced by 'Anthony Newley in The Small World of Gurney Slade' on his blog – it's easy to imagine people mistaking one for the other from the promotional material. Indeed, it's also possible that this played into the otherwise-confusing decision for ATV to repeat the series, a few months after the film was released).

Newley appeared in the film during the time he was also starring in *Stop The World...*, but other than the title and his appearance there's actually very little to connect this film, about a wheeler-dealer who works in a strip club and needs to collect £300 to pay off his gambling debts and avoid getting beaten up by gangsters, with the earlier series – although there is a scene early on in which Sammy is shaving and talks to himself, which is very reminiscent of **Gurney Slade**. As a film it's a good example of the genre (though full of characters expressing the misogyny and racism one would expect from 1960s gangsters), but a rather joyless one, whose only sympathetic character is repeatedly hurt by the film's protagonist.

It doesn't have much connection with **Gurney Slade**, but it seemed necessary to mention, at least in passing.

## Can Hieronymus Merkin Ever Forget Mercy Humppe And Find True Happiness?

This is possibly the oddest project Newley ever worked on. Co-written, co-produced, and directed by Newley, who also wrote the music and starred along with his then-wife Joan Collins (who played Polyester Poontang – this was not the most mature of films, in anything but its certification) and his children, this was a truly bizarre film, and very much in the same mould as **Gurney Slade**, though less successful.

Like Gurney, it used postmodernism and self-referentialism to straddle two very different genres – on the one hand it was a British sex comedy, of the kind that could easily be shelved next to the **Confessions Of...** series (or, at least, the more risque **Carry On** films or *Up Pompeii*), featuring Victor Spinetti and Bruce Forsyth, and with characters who included, as well as the eponymous Merkin and Mercy Humppe, Polyester Poontang, Filigree Fondle, and Goodtime Eddie Filth. On the other, it was an autobiographical attempt at an experimental film, which Roger Ebert called 'just about the first attempt in English to make the sort of personal film Fellini and Godard have been experimenting with in their very different ways[20]'.

Also like **Gurney**, it experiments wildly with different levels of reality and fiction within the same work. There is a film within a film within a film here – the film involves a film being made about the night in which Merkin shows a film he has made, which is (in some sense or another) also the film we are watching, which is also the film being made.

*Hieronymus Merkin* is, fundamentally, an unpleasant film, and it was also (according to Collins) partly responsible for destroying the Newley/Collins marriage, as she believed that some shots involving Newley's character having sex were not just acting. It's also, in many ways, an updating of *Stop The World...* – but the differences can be seen in the fact that while *Stop the World...* featured 'What Kind of Fool Am I?', *Hieronymus Merkin* featured a song called 'Oh What a Son of a Bitch I Am'. It's misogynist, and a sadly perfect crystallisation of the attitude towards women that had become common by that point in the 'sexual revolution'.

But at the same time, it's a film that's trying to do something different with the medium, and it even won the Writers Guild of Britain 'Best Original Screenplay' award. It's a unique work, and one that succeeds in its aim of capturing every aspect of its creator's personality – just unfortunately including the less salubrious ones.

## Fancy Wanders

Finally, we'll look at a sitcom written by Sid Green in 1980, which was the only time that either of the writers (rather than the star) of **The Strange World of Gurney Slade** returned to its themes. Indeed, that wasn't the only way in which this was Green returning to his earlier career, as the series starred Dave King, the comedian for whom Hills and Green had written at the very start of their career in the 1950s.

Unfortunately, it was not a particularly successful series, to the extent that it is almost impossible to track down a copy today – it

---

[20]https://www.rogerebert.com/reviews/can-heironymus-merkin-ever-forget-mercy-humppe-and-find-true-happiness-1969

was only broadcast once, and has never had a home video release of any description. It has also never (to my knowledge) turned up on any file-sharing sites devoted to vintage television – this is a series which, to all intents and purposes, no longer exists outside a handful of mentions on websites devoted to obscure comedy, and even there, it's usually only a couple of sentences along the lines of 'Sid Green wrote a sitcom which was a bit like **Gurney Slade** in 1980'.

I'm therefore not in a position to discuss it to the same extent as the other works listed here, which are at least accessible – I had just turned two when it was broadcast for the only time, and so have absolutely no memories of whether I saw it or not, and it seems largely forgotten even by those who saw it at an age where they could understand it, except that some of them say it was 'a bit like **Gurney Slade**' (and most of those people are basing this on their memories of both series on first broadcast, with nearly twenty years between them to forget the details). Unless and until it gets some sort of release – which seems vanishingly unlikely given the lack of interest in the series up to this point – it will be impossible to say how accurate those memories are.

This is a real shame, as at the moment, based on the evidence we have, the consensus position has always been that **Gurney Slade** was largely Newley's project, with Hills and Green acting more-or-less as ghostwriters. But it's entirely possible that getting a chance to view **Fancy Wanders** would give a totally different perspective on this, and may easily cause a re-evaluation of this position.

All of these works are, to the extent they're accessible, fascinating for the light they shed on the creators. But in the end, none of them properly recapture the true strangeness of **The Strange World of Gurney Slade**. And that seems an appropriate note on which to end.

# Bibliography

## Books

Bakhtin, Mikhail, tr. Emerson, Caryl, *Problems of Dostoevsky's Poetics*. Minneapolis, University of Minnesota Press, 1984. ISBN 9780816612284.

Bakhtin, Mikhail, tr. Iswolsky, Helene, *Rabelais and His World*. Boston, MIT Press, 1968. ISBN 9780262020374.

Barrett, William, *Irrational Man: A Study in Existential Philosophy*. New York, Doubleday, 1958. ISBN 9780385031387.

Beckett, Samuel, *Waiting For Godot: A Tragicomedy in Two Acts.* London, Faber & Faber, 1956.

Carroll, Lewis, *Alice's Adventures in Wonderland*. London, Macmillan, 1865.

Committee on Homosexual Offences and Prostitution, *Report of the Departmental Committee on Homosexual Offences and Prostitution*. London, Her Majesty's Stationery Office, 1957.

Gaines, William M. (ed.) *The Mad Reader*, London, Ballantine, 1954.

Swift, Jonathan, *Travels into Several Remote Nations of the World, in Four Parts: By Lemuel Gulliver, First a Surgeon, and then a Captain of Several Ships*. 1726. Revised ed, Dublin, George Faulkner, 1735.

MacInnes, Colin, *Absolute Beginners*. London, MacGibbon & Kee, 1959. ISBN 9780749005405.

Osborne, John. *The Entertainer*. Faber and Faber, London, 1957.

Willans, Geoffrey and Searle, Ronald, *The Compleet Molesworth*. London, Pavilion, 1990. ISBN 9781851450015.

Pirandello, Luigi, tr. Storer, Edward, *Six Characters in Search of an Author.* New York, E. P. Dutton, 1922.

Wilmut, Roger, From Fringe to Flying Circus, London, Eyre Methuen 1980, ISBN 9780413469502.

Wilson, Colin, *The Outside.*  London, Gollancz, 1958.

## Periodicals

*New Musical Express*. London, TI Media, 1952-2018.

       Murray, Charles Shaar, 'Gay Guerillas & Private Movies', cover date 24th February 1973.

## Television

*A Charlie Brown Christmas*, Lee Mendelsohn Films, 1965.

**The Adventures of Superman**, Motion Pictures for Television, 1952-58.

*Alice In Wonderland*. BBC, 1966.

**The Box of Delights**, BBC, 1984.

**Citizen James**, BBC, 1960-62.

       *Crusty Bread*, 1961.

       *The Jury*, 1962.

**Doctor Who**, BBC, 1963-

       *The Mind Robber*, 1968.

**EastEnders,** BBC, 1985-.

**Fancy Wanders**, LWT, 1980.

**The Frost Report**, BBC, 1966-7.

**Hancock**, BBC, 1961.

**Hancock's Half Hour**, BBC, 1956-60.

**Hollywood Squares**, Heather-Quigley Productions and others, 1966-2004.

**Monty Python's Flying Circus,** BBC, 1969-74.

**The Muppet Show,** ATV/ITC, 1976-82.

**That Was the Week That Was**, BBC, 1962-3.

**The Prisoner**, ITC, 1967.

**Q5**, BBC, 1969.

**Saturday Spectacular**, ATV, 1956-61.

**The Strange World of Gurney Slade**, ATV, 1960.

**Sunday Night at the London Palladium**, ATV, 1955-66.

**Two of a Kind**, ATV, 1961-68.

**Vision On**, BBC, 1964-76.

**Wagon Train**, Revue/Universal 1957-65.

# Film

Day, Robert, dir. *The Rebel*, Associated British Picture Corporation, 1961.

Fisher, Terrence, dir. *The Last Man to Hang?*, Association of Cinema Technicians, 1956.

Gilling, John, dir. *Idol on Parade*, Warwick Films, 1959.

Hamilton, Guy, dir. *Goldfinger*, EON 1964.

Hughes, Ken, dir. *The Small World of Sammy Lee,* Bryanston Films/Seven Arts Pictures, 1963.

Lean, David, dir. *Oliver Twist,* Cineguild, 1948.

Lester, Richard, dir. *A Hard Day's Night*, United Artists, 1964.

Lester, Richard and Sellers, Peter, dir. *The Running Jumping & Standing Still Film,* Peter Sellers Productions 1959.

Lumet, Sidney, dir. *Twelve Angry Men,* Orion-Nova Productions 1957.

Newley, Anthony, dir. *Can Heironymus Merkin Ever Forget Mercy Humppe And Find True Happiness?* Universal, 1969.

Saville, Philip, dir. *Stop the World, I Want to Get Off!* Warner Bros. 1966.

Stuart, Mel, dir. *Willy Wonka and the Chocolate Factory,* Wolper Pictures/The Quaker Oats Company, 1971.

## Music

### Vinyl Single

Derbyshire, Delia & Newley, Anthony, "Moogie's Bloogies"/"I Decoded You (Moogie's Bloogies pt. 2)" 2014, Trunk Records TTT008V.

### Audio CD

Bennett, Alan, Cook, Peter, Miller, Jonathan, and Moore, Dudley, *The Complete Beyond the Fringe*, EMI, 1996.

Kinks, the, *Something Else by the Kinks (Deluxe Edition)*, 1967 Pye, Castle Communications, 2011.

Kinks, the, *Preservation, Act 1,* 1973, UMC, 2010.

Newley, Anthony, *The UK Singles A's & B's and More: 1959-1962*, Jasmine Records, 2017.

Sellers, Peter, Collins, Joan, and Newley, Anthony, *Fool Britannia*, 1963, Acrobat 2008.

Small Faces, The, *Ogdens' Nut Gone Flake*, 1968, Sanctuary, 2012.

## Radio

**Beyond Our Ken**, BBC, 1958-64.

**The Goon Show**, BBC, 1951-60.

**Hancock's Half Hour**, BBC, 1954-9.

**Round the Horne**, BBC, 1965-8.

## Web

Banks, Clive, 'The Strange World of Gurney Slade' https://www.clivebanks.co.uk/Gurney%20Slade%20Intro.htm Accessed 02 April 2020.

Ebert, Roger, 'Can Heironymus Merkin Ever Forget Mercy Humppe and Find True Happiness?' https://www.rogerebert.com/reviews/can-heironymus-merkin-ever-forget-mercy-humppe-and-find-true-happiness-1969 Accessed 02 April 2020.

Fambrough, Preston, 'Ionesco's Rhinocéros and the Menippean Tradition', Studies in 20th & 21st Century Literature: Volume 34 Issue 1, Article 4. 2010. https://newprairiepress.org/cgi/viewcontent.cgi?referer=&httpsredir=1&article=1711&context=sttcl. Accessed 02 April 2020.

Idle, Eric, 'Influences', http://www.ericidle.com/blog/2016/04 Accessed 02 April 2020.

Kozloff, Sarah, 'Further Remarks on Showing and Telling', Cinema Comparat/ive Cinema, Volume 1 No.3 Words as Images, The Voice-Over. (2013). http://www.ocec.eu/cinemacomparativecinema/index.php/en/18-n-3-words-as-images-the-voice-over/156-further-remarks-on-showing-and-telling. Accessed 02 April 2020.

Letterboxd, 'The Strange World of Gurney Slade: Cast and Crew' https://letterboxd.com/film/the-strange-world-of-gurney-slade/crew/ Accessed 02 April 2020.

Mount, Paul, 'DVD Review: The Strange World of Gurney Slade' https://www.starburstmagazine.com/reviews/the-strange-world-of-gurney-slade. Accessed 07 April 2020.

'Re: The Strange World of Gurney Slade', https://www.cookdandbombd.co.uk/forums/index.php/topic,29303.msg1541792.html#msg1541792. Accessed 02 April 2020.

# Biography

Andrew Hickey is a writer, unsuccessful musician, and perennial third-place political candidate. When not losing elections he writes books on subjects including **Doctor Who**, superhero comics, 1960s harmony pop music, and the tenuous connections that can be found between those subjects if you look hard enough.

His first novel, *Faction Paradox: Head of State,* was published by Obverse Books in 2015, and his **Black Archive** on the **Doctor Who** serial *The Mind Robber* in 2016. He lives in Manchester with a very tolerant wife and a less tolerant Jack Russell.